Leonard Brown

Iowa

The Promised of the Prophets and other Patriotic Poems

Leonard Brown

Iowa
The Promised of the Prophets and other Patriotic Poems

ISBN/EAN: 9783337306892

Printed in Europe, USA, Canada, Australia, Japan

Cover: Foto ©Thomas Meinert / pixelio.de

More available books at **www.hansebooks.com**

IOWA

THE PROMISED *of the* PROPHETS,

AND OTHER

PATRIOTIC POEMS.

——BY——

LEONARD BROWN.

————§o§————

"There will be sung another golden age."
—*Bishop Berkeley.*

DES MOINES, IOWA:
CENTRAL PRINTING & PUBLISHING CO.,
1884.

CENTRAL PRINTING & PUBLISHING CO..
PRINTERS, Des Moines. Iowa.

To the enlightened, patriotic and generous "Old Settlers," who laid the foundation of Iowa's greatness on the everlasting granite of democratic liberty and the free common school,—and especially to the five hundred who have ordered copies of this little volume, in advance of its publication; and particularly to BARLOW GRANGER, JAMES CALLANAN, J. S. CLARKSON, BUREN R. SHERMAN, H. C HARGIS, THOS. MITCHELL, RESIN WILKINS, P. M. CASADY, GEORGE SNEER, SIMON CASADY, NATHAN ANDREWS, J, S. RUNNELLS, C. D. REINKING, WESLEY REDHEAD, HOYT SHERMAN, R. T. WELLSLAGER, M. P. TURNER, T. E. BROWN, J. S. POLK, P. H. BRISTOW, G. W. BRISTOW, C. A. MOSIER, AL. GREFE, M. H. LARSH, J. C. PAINTER, JNO. BECKWITH, E. R. MASON, N. R, KUNTZ, P. V. CAREY, BRUCE E. JONES, GEORGE W. DONNAN and JOHN A. KASSON for material assistance in the present undertaking; also, to JOHN YOUNGERMAN, WM. OSBORNE, ABE ASHWORTH. L. T. WOMACKS, J. O. MAHANA, E. R. CLAPP, B. F. ALLEN, D. M. BRINGOLF. J. H. McCLELLAND. G. A. STEWART WM, PORTER and the lamented A. S. VORSE, for help in my literary ventures of the past; and to J. A. NASH, JAMES SMITH, A. J. STEVENS, J. C, JORDAN, EDWARD McKENZIE, GIDEON BURGE, THOS. W. NEWMAN (of Burlington), SAMUEL GRAY, S. F. SPAFFORD, M. D. McHENRY, WM. H, McHENRY, P. H. BUZZARD. BENJ. BRYANT (deceased), my helpers in my school-boy days; and to my friends S. A. KELSEY, N. J. HARRIS, PETER NEWCOMER, GEO. W. HICKMAN, HALLETT & FULLER, the BAYLIES BROS., B F. BENNETT, AUG. SMITH, ISAAC BRANDT, H. H. GRIFFITHS, FRANK NAGLE, C. A. WEAVER, TAYLOR PIERCE, C. B. WORTHINGTON, the LAIRD BROS, the SKINNER BROS., G. M. WALKER, M. KAVANAUGH, SR., M. H. KING, A. CRAIG, H. R. HEATH, S. A. ROBINSON, an to all my well-wishers, the poem "IOWA" (immortal, if but a faint picture of our glorious State), is gratefully inscribed by

THE AUTHOR.

THE POET.

As mighty as the sun's meridian flame,
  Among the nations glows the poet's mind,.
  Enlightening and blessing all mankind.
How few have lived to merit his proud name !
Thy harp, O David, vibrates still on earth,
  Hymning melodiously Jehovah's praise ;
  Isaiah, thou thy voice in song didst raise ;
And Jeremiah, thine the poet's birth.
How high the honored calling of the Bard ;
  His God-given trust, how sacred and sublime!
Freedom and Truth and Virtue's watchful guard—
  A sentinel upon the tower of time,—
Yes Uriel in shining armor dressed,
Immortal honor beaming from his crest.

    July 4th, 1867.

PREFACE.

———o———

Part First of the poem that gives title to this volume was written twelve years after Iowa was admitted into the Union as a State; Part Second the following spring, and Part Third after an interval of twenty-two years. Part First recalls reminiscences of Iowa's "Past," giving a view of Indian life and manner ; Part Second extols her "Present" natural resources and scenery; and Part Third promises for Iowa in the near "Future" all that Isaiah pictures, or John of Patmos, or Virgil in his Fourth Eclogue, or Pope in his Messiah.

The "noble end"—the highest and holiest lessons on all topics vital to human welfare, can be reached by no "nobler means" than through the channel of verse. This form of writing, instead of being as many think artificial, is, on the contrary, the most truly natural. Every thing animate, whether plant or animal, is symmetrical. A tree is a written poem : its leaves are rhymes ; its flowers and fruit, melody ; and its mighty trunk, spreading branches and towering height, are strength, beauty and grandeur—all combined constitute true poetry. Every sentient being is a poem— man a sublime epic. But even inanimate nature does not always want symmetry—instance crystals, the planetary and stellary globes, drops of water, the rainbow and the plunging cataract—and where is not poetry found? Like the Infinite One, it is everywhere present.

What indeed is the proper aim of poetry? Let Hesiod answer who wrote "Works and Days," and Vir-

gil who wrote the "Georgics," and Lucan the author
of "Pharsalia," and Juvenal, and Lucretius, and even
Homer, greatest of all the ancient poets ; and let also
the old masters of English song speak : Dryden, Milton, Pope, Thompson, Young, Akenside, Beattie
Burns, and even Shakespeare, greatest of all poets.
They will reply : "*Its chief design* [the words of Dry-
den] *is to instruct.*" It is the hand-maiden of Virtue,
the guardian and protector of Liberty.

But, according to some canons of recent criticism,
poetry has not as its aim any "practical or material
utility " "Its aim," says a late author of a "Manual
of English Rhetoric," "is not to communicate knowledge or to influence the will ; but only to represent
products of creative imagination in their appropriate
forms in language." The author of the above defini-
tion is not a poet. No poet will admit any such doctrine to be true ; and Lord Kames, (the greatest writer on criticism that has lived since Quintilian,) says:
"Useful lessons conveyed to us in verse are agreeable
by the union of music with instruction ; but," he
adds, "are we to reject knowledge offered in a plainer
dress ? That would be rediculous; for knowledge is of
intrinsic merit, independent of the means of acquisition ; and there are many not less capable than willing to instruct us who have no genius for verse."
Here poetry is given its proper station above prose as
a means of education of mankind.

The good citizen and true poet (who must be a true
man) can perform no more sacred duty than to take
an absorbing interest in the affairs of his country and
age. So has the humble author of this little volume
ever done (thinking independently) and he has given
expression to his most cherished thoughts with an
earnestness suited to one who is by descent a Puritan,
and whose great-grandsire (he is proud to boast)
fought by the side of Putnam and Warren against the
British at Bunker Hill.

A dream of his in boyhood—a "vision of the night"
—has been an inspiration to him all his days. He
dreamed that he was in the same tent and in close
companionship with the "Father of his Country." It
would be offensively egotistical for him to give expression here to the faintest hope that his humble efforts with the pen—"mightier" (in the hands of the
favored of God and the good angels) "than the
sword"—could by any means give him a place in the
hearts of his countrymen by the [side of Washington.
But if his success could equal his ambition, he would
rescue his country from the dreadful condition of hu-
miliating slavery into which she has been plunged by
gold-bribed traitors, and he would place her feet
again upon the solid granite of freedom and independence.

Great Britain resolved to conquer America. She
has succeeded in fastening upon our people an interest
bearing debt—bonds and mortgages—amounting to
not less than twenty billions of dollars ; and thus she
exacts from us a vastly greater tribute than from all
her direct dependencies. Her agents were sent over
to prepare the way for our enslavement. Bonamy
Price, the Oxford professor, travelled extensively here,
lecturing in our principal cities and chief towns. He
spoke in Council Bluffs, Iowa, to the "grangers," telling them that "gold is the only money." Great
American statesmen, who had won the confidence of
our people during the civil war—trusted leaders North
and South—were gained over to the British interest.
The friends of American freedom and independence
uttered their patriotic protests in vain—unheeded by
the people, blinded by party spirit, and hoodwinked
by venal demagogues.

This little volume is the work of almost a life-time,
and the author will ever live conscious of having
striven to accomplish that which, if successful, will

be more to Iowa's honor and glory than even the new
Capitol, which (to the disgrace of either the building committee or of the State itself,) is to be decorated
within w th paintings executed, not by Iowa artists,
but by Italian. Oh, let the patriot hang down his
head in sorrow and shame, and never turn his eyes to
look upon the walls and ceilings of that costly building—a monument of the tax-gatherer's rapacity and
the shame of Iowa genius! Encourage Iowa talent
and leave the Italian to ply his vocation of artist in
Italy. Let the ceilings and walls of our public buildings exhibit only the handicraft of Iowa artists, and
let our public libraries be filled to overflowing with
the works of Iowa authors especially. This only is
patriotism, justice and right. Encourage Iowa poets
and artists, and Iowa will outrival very soon, in this
line of excellence, Italy and Greece. God has done
more for Iowa (the lovliest land embraced by the
grandest rivers) than for any other land on earth—let
her own people do their part to encourage Art and
Literature at home and her name will be exalted. But
costly theatres are being erected in every large town
in the State, and their walls and ceilings decorated
with all the gaudiness that money can purchase or
European fresco painters can daub on—for what purpose? to encourage fine art and literature—the hand-
maiden of religion and morality, for the education of
the people? No. Money is the sole end in view,—
behind all is avarice. A display of the legs of bra-
zen-faced harlots on the stage, is the enticing attrac-
tion the youth of Iowa are called upon to pay their
money to see, and shamelessly indecent colloquies to
hear recited. These schools of vice, joined with the
mirror-decorated wine and beer saloons and billiard
halls licensed by the State, and houses of prostituton
in every large town, winked at and encouraged by the
officers of the law, have about supplanted the church
of our fathers. If the patriot poet raise his indignant voice of protest against these evils that threaten
the life of society, give him, O reader a kindly hear-
ing.

LEONARD BROWN.

DES MOINES, IOWA, Dec, 15, 1883

CONTENTS.

———o———

POESY.

—o—

Is Poesy, then, only garden flowers
    That, cultivated with a kindly care,
    With beauty glow, and sweetly scent the air,
And lovers languish in the leafy bowers?
'Tis might,—behold the dreaded lion cowers
    (Before the strong man) smitten in his lair:
    See the fierce Norman slay the Russian bear.
'Tis beauty not unlike the smiling Hours!
'Tis might and beauty gracefully combined—
    See Dian in the groves with bow and quiver;
She slays the tusky boar, pursues the hind;
    She views her radiant tresses in the river;
The blameless beauty blesses all mankind—
    Yea, God to man of Poesy's the giver!

    July, 1865,

IOWA.

PART FIRST.

(1858.)

This piece (Iowa, Part First,) was written after the Author's return to Polk county from school at Burlington, Iowa. He spent the spring and summer of 1858 under the shelter of his father's humble log-cabin roof at Saylor's Grove. His "study" was the woods, where he walked, composing rhymes, until he made a well-beaten path under the shadow of beautiful trees. This composition is, perhaps, the most polished of any of the Author's verses—too great license of alliteration being indulged, as the reader will observe. He took his pictures of Indian life from a little work entled "The Life of Blackhawk."

The lines of seven and eight syllables are after the manner of many English poems written in the eighteenth century, the "Ode to Solitude" by Granger, and "Grongar Hill," by Dyer, being examples of this style of versification.

IOWA.

———o———

THE PAST.

A MORNING'S MEDITATION ON THE BANKS OF THE DES MOINES.

"Every human heart is human."—LONGFELLOW.

It is a pleasant summer morn;
Gently waves the growing corn;
Erom the leafy groves, the air
Wafts a fragrance everywhere ;
And along the eastern sky
Lovely sunbeams greet the eye,
That o'er fairy clouds diffuse
Tinges of unnumbered hues.
At length the Sun himself appears,
Great herald of revolving years !
And smiles as radiant and young
As when immortal Ossian sung !
Thou giver of the lovely day !
From thee I turn my face away;
I cannot for a moment brook
Thy searching glance thy piercing look ;
But gladly on this stream I gaze,

From which thy ever-splendent rays
Have driven the mists, that o'er it spread
Dark as the living cloud so dread
That hovered o'er a pleasant land
As one of old "stretched out his hand."
I love upon these banks to stray
Thus at the sweet approach of day,
And gazing on the beautious stream ·
To wander in poetic dream.
I hear a distant lonely sound,
That carries sadness all around!
'Tis of the ever mournful dove
Sighing for her absent love.
Here let me recline my head
Pensive on this mossy bed,
Nearer by the river side,
Where waters murmur as they glide,—
That my ear may catch again
The ever tender, saddening strain;
For it moving, moaning on
Recalls to mind the loved ones gone,
Whom bright angels bore away
To realms of everlasting day.
Now there comes a deeper moan;
'Tis sadder than a dying groan!
The waves are sighing as they flow,—
Methinks are singing as they go,
A mournful melancholy lay,—
The dirge of a departed day.

SONG OF THE WAVES.

The dead! The dead! The dead are here!
Ask not the day, ask not the year,
When loved ones bore them on the bier,
And laid them lowly in the ground.
And made the monumental mound!
Age hath followed ages fast;
The streams new channels formed and past,
And deep through rocks have worn their way
Since they mouldered into clay:

    The patriot brave who thoughtful stood
    Looking down upon this flood;
    His country's wrongs were in his breast;
    Eye-flashing rage his look expressed,
    Revenge resolving on her foes—
    His blood redeemed her from her woes;
    Rest thee, O warrior, in repose!

The lovely maid who oft of yore
Gathered wild flowers on this shore,
Strolling in the happy grove,
Caroling a song of love;
Now bathing in the limpid waves;
Now in the cooling breeze she laves,
And gazing, like fair Eve, with pride
In the pellucid mirror-tide,
Viewing there her form and face,
All radiant with every grace,
She modestly and sweetly smiled,—

Behold her, Nature's lovely child!
She sleeps in death, low in the ground,
Beneath the ancient grassy mould.

And the Bard, (whose song was given--
A light to guide from Earth to Heaven)—
There lies, with harp beneath his head,
Unstrung, decayed; its voice is dead!
To all resistless was its spell,
While sang the aged Minstrel
The sylvan beauties of these streams;
The hero's wondrous deeds and dreams;
Love's longing looks, and soul-born smiles;
Her hidden hopes, and winsome wiles.
And shall its strains no more arise
Rejoicing to these western skies,
As wild birds sing, and waters flow,
And lovely prairies verdant grow?

O stream, how touching is thy lay!
And must great worth thus find decay,
And all man's glory fade away?

THE INDIAN.

From thee has gone the Indian brave;
Nor Sac, nor Fox beholds thy wave;
And yet upon thy margin green
Not long ago his lodge was seen,
In its wild, fantastic form,—
An humble covert from the storm;
His trembling maize field stood hard by;

His bean-and-melon-patch was nigh;
His pony fed upon the plain,—
See all the Indian had of gain!
And well content, when thus supplied;
His every want was satisfied;
His happy heart, with love of gold,
Had not begun to rot or mould;
The needy stranger at the door
Was welcome to the red man's store.

I have often in delight
Seen the meteor at night,
With a glorious display,
Darting hurridly away
Across the star-bespangled sky,
Joying in its course on high;
It soon vanished from my view,
Buried in the boundless blue,
Leaving not a trace behind
Of the glory it resigned.

The Indian passed away, and lo!
What is left behind to show
That he drew Ulysses' bow?
He often earned immortal fame;
But what perpetuates his name?
What monument remains to tell
Where, like Leonidas, he fell?
Many an unknown field may be
A Marathon or Thermopylæ!

2

All he for ages said or did
Must ever lie in darkness hid;
Only here a grassy sod
Marks where once his wigwam stood,
And some little pits remain
That in winter held his grain.
The sweet flowing "Chicaqua," *
And the bright "Asipala," †
Lost are these names to rivers clear;
While the ruder ones we hear
Ungrateful to the poet's ear!
Still round the graves, and o'er the dead
Some mossy bark and boards are spread;
It was of these the mourners made
A little wigwam for his shade,
To be for it a sheltering home,
Until he o'er the prairie roam,
And, wandering find the rolling flood,
That flows this side the happy wood—
The ever-joyful hunting ground
In which exhaustless game is found.
There—if his course of life had been
Bright and free from trace of sin—
He would cross the trembling log
With his ever faithful dog,
And join his comrades in the chase,
And live in endless happiness;
If like the hound, he come there hoarse
From baying on a vicious course,
He cannot reach the happy wood,

*Skunk River.   †Raccoon River.

But quickly falls into the flood;
Then rolling, howling, in the tide,
He struggles for the nearest side,—
Every effort is in vain,
To reach the woodland or the plain;
The rushing wave, with mighty roar,
Sweeps him to a barren shore ;—
Degraded there in poverty,
He finds eternal misery.

Meandering the prairies green
Still the Indian path is seen,
Bending over wooded hills,
Crossing sweetly flowing rills.
Wandering near it thoughtfully,
Imagining most pleasantly,
Rare visions of the fairest kind,
Came on bright before my mind.

A CEREMONY.

I saw a long, lamenting train
Of women passing o'er the plain,
Appearing as they had before
Annually in days of yore;
Moaning matrons moving on,
And weeping widows, one by one ;
Sorrowing sisters were the last
In the procession as it passed —

So very sad; and yet, I ween,
There never was a lovelier scene
Than they presented to my sight,
Performing this religious rite,
Of bearing gifts, and proffering
To their dead an offering;
All the maidens passed along
Chanting wild and mournful song.

THE INDIAN MAIDS' SONG.

"Again returns the day of sadness!
Again returns the day of gladness!
The Great Spirit has bereft us;
The Great Spirit has not left us;
Friends are gone; nor do we greet them;
Friends are gone; but we shall meet them;
Good Spirits hover o'er us lightly;
Good Spirits shine above us brightly;
From the rocks and caves they started;
From the rocks and caves departed,
When they heard us weeping, moaning, —
When they heard us sighing, groaning;
On their swan-like wings came fleeting;
On their swan-like wings came greeting —
Greetiug us , and now are near us;
Greeting us with words to cheer us:
'Weep no more; be not fearful;
Weep no more; be calm and cheerful —
The Great Spirit loves you dearly;

The Great Spirit knows how nearly
His good children are unto him;
His good children all shall view him;
View him and dwell with him ever;
View him and be parted never;
Never more shall sigh in sorrow;
Never more shall dread the morrow!
Let this, then, be day of gladness;
Let it not be one of sadness;
Weep no more; be not fearful;
Weep no more; be calm and cheerful'!"

And appearing truly fair,
With their zephyr combed hair
Flowing over shoulders bare,
And the dark expressive eye,
Hopeful turned towards the sky, —
Angel form; romantic dress;
They were queens in lovliness!
Now all have reached the burial place,
And there I can more clearly trace
The deepening of their wild distress, —
The dead they mournfully address!·
The mother thus:—

        " My babe so dear!
My little darling, Oh, come near;
Let me again behold thy face,
And with fond kisses thee embrace!
Something I see most lovely, fair,

And bright, above me in the air, —
'T is sure, 't is sure my very child!
Come nearer still, thou vision mild,
And never, never more depart!
Oh, could I press thee to my heart!
Thanks, thanks to Onwenah above,
Who thus would spare thee in his love,
To calm thy mother's stormy breast,
To give her wearied spirit rest;
For now, no more, no more I weep!
My soul with rapture glories deep;
Since I behold on wings of light,
My child so beautiful and bright!

The widow : —

          "O, my husband, why,
Why wilt thou not descend from high,
And to my sorrowing soul convey
Of thy bright joy a single ray!
Forlon, forlon, I here must be!
O dearest, dearest, pity me,
And take me once again to thee!
Enwrap me in thy arms once more,
And on the bright celestial shore,
Where nothing in immortal groves
May ever more distract our loves!
O husband! when with flagging pace
Thou art returning from the chase,
Oppressed with toil; thy arrows spent;

Thy back with fleshy burden bent;
Who now doth strain her anxious sight
To see thee gain the woody height,
And, when thy shadow there doth stray,
So soon is on her willing way
To bear a part of thy dull load
And lead thee to the fair abode,
Where viands for thee she hath blest,
That thou may'st eat and sweetly rest?
And when thou liest wrapped in sleep
Doth o'er thee midnight vigil keep,
And, as the moon, serenely bright,
Enchants the wigwam with her light—
Reveals the features of thy face,
Who doth thee lovingly embrace?

" Brothers, [thus the sisters said,]
  Return from wandering with the dead!
  Receive this offered gift of ours;
  Receive these lovely prairie flowers!
  We lay them gently on the tomb
  To please you with their sweet perfume;
  They are the fairest we can find
  Disporting in the prairie wind!
  On plucking them they seemed to say,
' We gladly go with you away
  To form the happiest bouquet!
  A token, beautiful, of love
  From friends below to friends above.'
  And other presents, too, we bring

With this our kindly offering —
Your bow and arrows here we place ;
For you may need them in the chase;
And your ornaments so fair,
We now leave them in your care.
On your graves no wilding grows.
Pebbles mark where you repose;
Pebbles that to-day we took
From the gently flowing brook;
And above you they are spread
As on the silvery minnow's bed.
Here we also leave you food ;
For it is a weary road
You again must travel o'er
Ere you reach the happy shore. "
This said, the radiant vision fair
Vanished quickly into the air.

THE TWO BROTHERS.

And then two youths of gentle mien
Went gliding by me o'er the green,
Who so great beauty had, and grace,
And loveliness in form and face,
That, (as I had not long before
Been glancing into ancient lore)
I thought of Æneas goddess born !
How he, when cast away, forlorn,
Upon the Carthagenian strand,

Did first before Queen Dido stand,
Delivered from the misty cloud
That hid him from the busy crowd,—
How beauty sparkled in his eyes,
Beauty descended from the skies!
The goddess curled his flowing hair;
Gave him youthful vigor rare;
Crowned his brow with ambient light;
Made his face serenely bright,
Like polished ivory beauteous bold,
Or Parian marble gemmed with gold.
I thought of fair Apollo, too,
With his far-shooting silver bow,
And golden quiver, glittering bright,
And arrows dipped in healing light,—
God of benevolence and truth;
The god of beauty and of youth—
Immortal, glorious, fearless, young—
Sweet his heavenly lyre rung;
The soul of harmony he fired;
The silent muses he inspired.
Would thou, my Muse, by him were taught,
Had spark of heavenly fire caught,
Like sirens on the lonely isle,
To charm the passer-by awhile,
That he might lend attentive ear
This story from thy lips to hear—
(Of no imaginary act,
But well-authenticated fact)
Of love two youths each other bore—

So great as seldom known before!
They brothers were, and they were *men*;
And true they were not " white;" but then
'T is not the color of the skin
That tells us of the heart within.
They lived together; hunted game;
And, beside, they thought of *fame*.
However much men in their talk,
The love of glory seem to mock,
Should they the truth in candor own,
Would gladly have their own names known;
For 't is a feeling, and confest,
Which dwells in almost every breast
From that of humblest of the earth
To those of highest rank and birth.
And God himself—Ancient of Days!—
Commands that men shall sing his praise.
Who would not, like the Condor, seek
To gain the Andes' loftiest peak,
Could he thence on wings arise,
And soar toward the azure skies
And pass pale Cynthia in his flight,
And on the morning star alight,
And there amid effulgence dwell
For longer time than tongue can tell?
No labors are for man too hard
Where renown is the reward;
For this did Raphael command
The pencil with untiring hand;
For this Beethoven, deaf and old,

Unwrapped sheet music's every fold;
For this blind Milton sought in song,
And toiled so deep, and toiled so long!
The love of praise raised up, we know,
Demosthenes and Cicero;
'T was this that fashioned the "Greek Slave;"
'T was this made Bonaparte so brave.
Among Red Men the surest way
To honor, is the foe to slay;
Him they call supremely great
Who can most martial deeds relate.
The brothers, then, we cannot blame
For feeding the heroic flame.
The elder, chasing deer one day
Beyond the praries, far away,
Came where the hunting-ground he saw
Of the long hated Dakota;
Before his mind rose every one
Of all the wrongs that had been done
By that dread people to his own, —
(His aged father they had slain,
Whilst he was passing o'er the plain,
And e're they let his soul depart,
Tore from his breast his bleeding heart,
And, fiend-like, laughed to see it pant,—
On high they flung it for a taunt!)
Could he restrain his raging ire, —
From his veins expel the fire, —
As appeared distinct in view
One that seemed the savage Sioux?

"Be true," said he, "my trusty bow,
Lay the abhorred villian low!
And then an arrow keen he took;
With flint 't was pointed from the brook;
And feathered from the eagle's wing;
And bound around with sinew string.
The bow he drew with mighty force;
The dart went hissing on its course,
Unseen, so swift it winged the air;
He saw it seek the bosom bare;
And, though afar it then had sped,
He saw the blood come gushing red.
The victim threw his hands on high
And sunk upon the turf to die;
The victor made exulting shout —
A foe was slain he had no doubt.
O youth, what fate must thee attend,
Should it not prove a foe; but *friend?*
Now with an eager haste he ran,
And stood above the dying man,
And stooping down, the scalp to take,
(A trophy for his honor's sake,)
When lo, instead of hated *Sioux,*
The friendly *Iowa* he knew!
He paused: the knife fell to the ground;
He drew the arrow from the wound.
Like the stern commander bold
Who by the messenger is told,
" The city of deserved hate
Will on no terms capitulate;

But dare unto the latest hour
With deadly scorn defy his power."
Anger rushes to his face;
He cries aloud, " The mortars place;
For she shall yield in dire disgrace !"
Ten thousand comets, as it were,
Soon are flaming in the air,
As if their course had wrathful fled
To descend upon her head!
Death and Destruction reign around;
And mighty Ruin strews the ground!
Behold! her gates she opens wide;
The hero enters them in pride!
His plume is waving in the wind;
His soldiers follow him behind;
High he holds his peerless head;
Beneath his feet he spurns the dead;
Until he finds — now free from pain —
A lovely lady 'mong the slain —
Sweetly wrapped in death — at rest —
A smiling infant on her breast.
Behold the hero bowing low!
Adown his cheek the warm tears flow!
He takes the babe upon his arm,
And saves the innocent from harm.
And so the youth; how his heart bled!
How fain would he have raised the dead!
Alas! he finds his grief too late;
So firm are the decrees of fate!
Before those eyes a darkness rose;

The spirit sought a long repose.
Awhile he stands in mute suspense ;
Then with a tender eloquence :—
" And thou hast found the spirit land,
Sent by an undesigning hand ;
My hopes with thine are at an end ;
For this my death must make amend."
And then his way he homeward bent,
Soliloquizing as he went :—
" ' No, he did it purposely,
And to escape doth falsify,'
Thus will they answer my defense,
When I avow my innocence
Of having murdered by design.
I planly see what fate is mine,
And to the same myself resign.
Some months had passed, when men were
 sent
Him to demand for punishment ;
And they found him on his bed ;
Disease had humbled low his head ;
Yet willing was, at their command,
To rise and seek the foreign land ;
And their unfeeling orders were,
" By coming morn he should prepare
With them to go upon the way ;
Or ill or well, he must obey."

THE INDIAN VILLAGE.

A lovely " Iowa " village stood
Within the shadow of a wood,
And by the margin of a stream;
How happy did its people seem!
Around the council-house behold
A great concourse of young and old!
Is not the purpose of the throng
The avenging of a wrong?
And was the youth torn from his bed,
And here before accusers led?
A youth of humble modesty
Within the council-house we see;
Such beauty brightening in his face
As would well an angel grace;
Reclining lowly on the ground,
While chiefs and braves with look profound,
Are seated in a circle round.
Behold the leading chief arise!
Now on the youth he rests his eyes,
And thus he speaks in accents slow:—
" Ere this the just avenging blow
Deep in the dust hath laid you low;
But ancient custom of our land,
Bids that you first before us stand,
With privilege of self defense
With all you have of eloquence."
And so, the youth rose from the ground,

And cast a pleasant look around;
Then from his robe freed his right arm,
And stood erect, nor in alarm.
All eyes surveyed the brave young man,.
As with sweet accent he began :—

"Fathers! I have my death-song sung;
    With joy my voice in numbers rung;
    For as I came along to die,
    I heard the honey-bee flit by ;
    Its course it turned toward the sky.
    Methought it spake my spirit so :—
'Arise, arise, from fields below
    To where the sweeter flowers blow!
    Their cups of bliss to thee no more
    Shall close upon the happy shore.'
Wherefore grim Death, then, should I fear ?
    My own free choice doth bring me here!
    It is not, Fathers! my desire
    That words shall mitigate your ire ;
    The tom'hawk cn my head must fall ;
    Nor this may I injustice call ;
    It would not now the stroke prevent
    To claim my brother innocent
    Of having with vile purpose slain
    One of your braves upon the plain.
Fathers ! here I take the place
    Of him whom you would now disgrace ;
    Into your hands my life I give ;
    O, that my brother long may live !

Upon his bed he lies, too ill
Himself your mandate to fulfill !
I came without his own consent,
And much he strove me to prevent;
Such has his kindness to me been
Would I NOT die for him, 't were sin."

Thus having said, again he sate
Him down among these men of state,
And there awaited calm his fate.
Did they arise with furious yell,
Bend over him like fiends of hell,
Bury the tom'hawk in his brain,
And bid him sleep, nor wake again ?
Ah no, full glad am I to say
How well they welcomed him that day !
They freely gave the friendly hand,
And bade him with the bravest stand ;
And then resolved to make a feast
In honor of the worthy guest !
So, down into the glen they go,
Hard by the rivulet below,—
I trow, no fairer spot of ground
In all the boundless West is found !
Dame Nature there has carpet spread,
The giant oaks nod overhead ;
'Neath craggy rock is sylvan spring,
Near which by moonlight maidens sing ;
Nor distant hence afar is found
A spacious grot beneath the ground

3

Where oft young men and maids repair,
And presents in their hands they bear
For the good spirit that dwells there.
Then as the dusky eve draws nigh,
They seek a mossy seat hard by,
Where they may catch the lovely sound
Of water as it trickles down
From a shelving rock above;
Here they sit and talk of love;
And oftentimes prolong their stay
While Hesperus crowns departing day,
And after she has long sought rest
On her couch low in the west.
A deep-worn circle, too, is seen,
Near by the spring, upon the green,
Where now young braves are chanting loud
And aged warriors, bold and proud—
(All painted o'er with many a hue;
And each a hieroglyphic true—
Telling of the foes they slew)
Are dancing many an antic round,
To rudest instrumental sound;
Waving the war-club oft on high
Or pointing arrows to the sky,
Portraying how they battles gained,
Or how the bison's blood they drained,
Or how the bow, from crag on high,
Brought down the eagle bold to die.
All the village throng is there,—
The young, the old, the brave, the fair,

So that now under every tree
A group there is in gladsome glee!
Participating in the sport,
Their guest is happy as at court!
Meanwhile are matrons hurrying fast
To prepare the rich repast.
Soon, at a well-known signal, all,
Male and female, great and small,
Place themselves in order round,
Low seated on the grassy ground;
While those that are of high degree
On elevated mound we see—
A place of greater dignity—
And honored far above the rest,
We may behold the youthful guest.
To him they first refreshment bring,
And then to others of the ring
Promiscuously, till soon 't is known
That well supplied is every one;
When with great joy they all partake
Of bounteous gift of wood and lake;
Of maize-bread, product of the soil;
But most of fruit of huntsman's toil,—
The flesh of buffalo and bear;
Of the elk and of the deer;
And fish—the pike and salmon rare—
All that fair Nature here affords
Graces this banquet of her lords;
Much of the fruit of vine and tree
And honey of the working bee.

How sweet a nectar, too, they bring
From the ever-bubbling spring!
Bubbling from the sands below—
Sands as pure and white as snow!
How happy was the feast, and long;
And echoed oft the hills with song—
Song of welcome to the stranger—
Welcome there, all free from danger!

A SONG OF WELCOME.

Welcome, stranger, welcome here!
Thou art welcome to our cheer!

Has he not a loving brother,
    And may be a sister dear,
And an old heart-broken mother,
    And an aged father near,
Who are now bowed down in sorrow
    For this loved one good and brave,
Fearing lest the coming morrow
    Find him slumbering in the grave?

Do not think our eyes so blinded;
    Do not think our souls so vile;
Do not think us so dark minded;
    Do not think us lost in guile,
That we cannot see, all glowing!
    Light—a spark from God above!
Or seeing, and its purpose knowing,
    Would stifle such a light of love!

Welcome, stranger, welcome here !
Thou art worthy of our cheer!

The sun his face began to hide
Within the vast Pacific tide,
Ere they the village reach again,
Where all seek rest save the young men,
They on their coursers ride afar
While lingers the bright evening star.
It was indeed a lovely sight
To look upon them by moonlight,
Dashing through woods and over plains—
Without saddle, without reins !
Now all meeting in one place,
  Loud neigh the horses for the race ;
The riders bending forward then,
Their coursers (more than ten times ten)
Spring onward with a mighty bound;
  The prairies tremble far around ;
And thundering hoofs on air resound.
  They speed, they speed full fast away !
  But see two steeds of glossy bay—
How sweet the moonbeams on them play !
They leave the others far behind—
Much like the Anglo-Saxon mind
In great achievements for mankind.

The night is past, bright morning glows;
And all have had a calm repose ;
And they have said their fervent prayers

To Him who ever for them cares,—
(To whom devotedly they pray,
At morn and eve of every day).
Now, ere the stranger guest depart,
They show again a kindly heart.
By making presents to him there,
Which he may with his brother share :
Two good suits of hunters' clothes,
Two wampum belts, and two strong bows ;
Then many of their dearest beads ;
And last, the pair of bright bay steeds,
Which on the happy eve before
In the race had triumph bore!

He, joyful went to greet his brother ;
Long they lived to love each other.

THE CONCLUSION.

And now, fair stream, have I mused long,
And lengthened out a thankless song !
It is thy fault, sweet stream, I say,
That I have wandered so away!
Why do the lovely sunbeams lave
And glisten in thy rippling wave ?
Why do the willows on thy brink
Bow down their heads and seem to drink ?
Why does the pretty "silver-side"
Play through thy waters so in pride ?
Had never these my vision crossed

Perhaps I had not now been lost!
Why is that venerable mound
Upon thy level margin found?
Who made it thus of earth and stone
To thee, O ancient stream, 'tis known!
I look upon it, and my mind
In thought no resting-place can find;
I think that it, perhaps, was built
Where blood, a deluge, had been spilt;
Perhaps, beneath where it arose
Bones of a patriot repose;
While this alone by it is told,—
"*A people dwelt here once of old;*"
And seems to mention with the same,—
"*They dwelt here ere the Indian came.*"
The Indian! Keokuk the great!
Pride of a patriotic State!
In battle, braver ne'er was one;
In wisdom, the bright noonday sun;
In eloquence, a crowned king,—
Surpassed by none in anything
That can exalt a Red Man's name
And give to him undying fame!
No power so strong—no base-born bribe—
Could lead him to betray his tribe.
Be ye reproved, vile statesmen old,
Who love your country less than gold!
"*I liked my towns—my corn fields, too:*
For these, O white man, I fought you!"

Thus speaks the wronged Indian dead ;
'Twas thus the patriot Black Hawk said.
Be long, my lovely Iowa, be
Home of as noble-hearted free !

Thou stream, farewell !   I shall be lorn
'Till smiling dawns another morn,
When here I once again may stray
And while an happy hour away !

SAYLOR'S GROVE, JUNE, 1858.

IOWA.

PART SECOND.

(1859.)

IOWA. (Part Second), is an attempt to paint pleasing pen-pictures of natural scenery—a most difficult undertaking. In this Poesy and Painting come near each other and become entitled to be called "Twin Sisters."

The pleasant Spring of 1859, spent in Saylor's Grove, like the Spring and Summer before, were halcyon days to the young writer. Then his hopes were brightest. But the dreams of youth are often wilted by the frosts of later life. There is this compensation, however: Our disappointments are a school-master to us. If we, (like Socrates and Tasso) are under the protection of some heavenly guardian and are predestined, (like Joseph) to be a benefactor of our kindred and countrymen, the way to success lies not necessarily along pleasant paths, nor can the persecuting jealousy of little men prevent our final triumph.

IOWA.

——o——

THE PRESENT.

A MORNINGS MEDITATION ON THE BANKS OF THE DES MOINES.

*"Let all the ends thou aimest at be thy country's,
Thy God's, and truth's."*—SHAKSPEARE.

I now the wished-for morn behold ;
The sun displays his crown of gold ;
But many smiling days have flown,
The dove hath uttered many a moan,
Since I, reclining here alone,
Mused in melancholy mood,
As the sorrowful Past I viewed.
Let my thoughts this morning be
From all melancholy free ;
Indeed, the Present gives my mind,
Of images a pleasing kind ;
And the Future meets my view
Illumined with a golden hue.

Are not these Western streams as fair
As Tiber, Thames, the Seine, or Ayr,

Danube, Vistula, Guadalquivir,
Or any European river ?
If e'en to Asia I should go,
And there behold the Hoang-ho,
Euphrates, Indus, Irawaddy,
Bramapootra, and Cambodia ;
And stray through Africa awhile—
Behold the Niger and the Nile—
When from my wanderings I come
And view again the streams at home,
I ask, would these not seem to me ·
As fair as those beyond the sea ?
Iowa, virgin State, is seen
Arrayed now in her robes of green—
A maid of more than mortal charms—
Diana in two happy arms,
As if from high come down again
To fair Endymion of men.
The river on her eastern side
Exalts my patriotic pride !
It needs no sounding trump of fame
To send abroad the well known name.
The British bard would glad depart
From the monotony of Art,
Displayed before him all the while,
Upon his much loved native Isle,
Where hedges white in May, as snow
Checker the land where'er he go,—
The flowery scene is fair, I know;
But Nature, wild and primitive,

There no longer seems to live,
Right glad would he depart, I say,
On Mississippi's banks to stray.
Along Iowa's western side
Flows the Missouri deep and wide,—
Rivers beautiful and great
Are the pride of any State;
And who will question this so true,
That Iowa hath not a few?
Hers are the great and little Sioux,
The Turkey ahd Makoqueta,
Red Cedar; and the Iowa,
Besides "wide-bottomed" Chicaqua,—
Asipala (or swift Raccoon)
And many more, with which the Doon
And the far-renouned Ayr
In length nor beauty can compare.
But for good reason have I passed
By thee, Des Moines, to name thee last:
However distant I may roam,
I find no place I love like home;
And towns and cities I have seen
Exceeding beautiful, I ween,
But I prefer my village still,
Which I behold on yon green hill;
Her damsels seem to me more fair
Than those I ever meet elsewhere.
For some good reason do I love
More than all others this my grove;
High on yon bending hickory

The squirrel often speaks to me;
Here on an evening calm and still
I hear the lonely whip-poor-will;
While frequently I all day long
Sit listening to continual song,—
A choir chanting in this wood
A chorus to the praise of God,
Who hath sent Winter far away
And ushered in the vernal May.
All creatures seem thus to rejoice,
Without but one discordant voice.
From beak of little warbling bird
Hath any person ever heard.
(Although his locks be white with years)
"This world is but a vail of tears?"
No, no, its little speech is this:—
"Behold our world, a world of bliss!"
It is indeed a very shame;
It is blaspheming God's high name,
Who built the starry dome above,
Who filled the universe with love,
Crowned Beauty as a queen to reign,
O'er all His glorious domain,
That any creature can be heard
To contradict the little bird!
Yes, the happy warblers sing
To welcome in the days of Spring—
And what a merry, merry lay!
How it delights my mind to-day
While on these pleasant banks I stray.

Ah, Des Moines, need I now tell,
Why 'tis I like thy shores so well?

Once musing on thy banks, O stream,
I had a memorable dream!
A beauteous maid before me stood;
She seemed a huntress of the wood;
And I beheld her bow unstrung;
Her quiver o'er her shoulder hung;
I saw not e'en an arrow there;
Around it wantoned her long hair;
Her dress seemed loosely o'er her placed,
Except 'twas girdled round her waist;
Nor shoes had she upon her feet;
Her eyes so bright knew not deceit;
A lovely wreath of flowers hung
Around her neck; and them she flung,
With kindly smile, about my own;
Then meekly on a mossy stone
She sat her down, but not alone;—
It did not seem to wound her pride
That I should seat me by her side;
But now she looks on me in love;
She seems an angel from above!
Ah, now she passes from my view,—
Glides swiftly in a bark canoe,
Toward thy northern shores, fair stream;
And much I sorrow in my dream!
I see thy sparkling waves full plain;
She dips her paddle in again;

The trees behold the swift canoe,
And wave to her a kind adieu ;
The birds now chant a mournful lay,
That she must pass from them away ;
The woods and prairies grieve full 'sore,
That they shall see her face no more ;—
Her every movement seems to tell,
In beauty none can her excel ;
And what a voice was hers—so clear !
Methinks its accents now I hear
While she glides gracefully along,
Still carroling her farewell song.

FAREWELL SONG OF PRIMITIVE NATURE.

The Sun shall continue in his kindly duty
  Through days without number to come,
Of rising and painting this landscape with beauty,
  Then gliding with joy to his home.

And oft will he pass by the twelve constellations
  That encircle the heavens above ;
And Spring shall respond to his kind invitations,
  And be seen here as oft in her love.

The beautiful Summer, Autumn fruit-laden,
  And white-bearded Winter severe,
Will return like a youth at the beck of a maiden,
  Whene'er he shall bid them appear.

Sable Night, as if wrapped in a robe of deep
    mourning,
Will stalk here in sadness and gloom,
Till the moon shall arise with her silver adorn-
    ing,
Like a spirit goes up from the tomb.

The stars gladly join her with beauty refulgent,
    Like eyes when they sparkle with mirth;
Thick clouds are all banished; for winds were
    indulgent,—
Behold now a glorious earth!

I leave this loved land; but I go not in sorrow;
    I bid now adieu to this shore;
My sister comes after to dwell here to-mor-
    row,—
Sweet land, shall I see thee no more?

The storm-cloud shall rise from the West with
    its thunder
    Deep-echoing terror afar;
The three-forked lightning shall cleave oaks
    asunder,—
    Dread shaft from a furious star.

When these plains are uplifted by volcanic fires
    That sleep now in quiet below,
And pierce the high clouds with the rock-poin-
    ted spires
    Encased in perpetual snow;

4

When these rivers have fled and are lost in the
    ocean;
Nor their trace can we longer discern;
And all things are changed in the mighty com-
    motion,
    Behold once again I return!

    As this one vanishes from sight
    Behold another vision bright!
    Another maid approaching me,—
    Hers is the voice of "Liberty."

A SONG OF "LIBERTY."

    Nature and I twin sisters are,
      We love alike the wilderness;
    But still we wander oft afar,
      And give to Art her mightiness.

    'T is I the souls of men inspire
      With longings for immortal fame;
    I kindle in their breasts the fire;
      I fan it to a mounting flame.

    Cast but a glance at ancient Greece;
      Whose strength exalted her so high?
    In war the mightiest; in peace
      She seems uplifted to the sky!

    'T was Liberty gave her her men;
      Her men created her renown;

But can I not call up again
    As great as wore the olive crown?

Another age, another clime,
    Where Tyranny ne'er drew a breath,
May yet behold a scene sublime,—
    The mighty, as though raised from death.

Raised freed as from their former clay,—
    Debasing passions laid aside,—
Raised to enjoy a full-orbed day,
    And feel a more becoming pride.

Protected by the one true God
    Whom they with reverence behold;
They'll walk in paths before untrod,
    And darkest mysteries unfold.

This lovely land they'll re-create,—
    Make Eden bloom on earth once more;
Here, here will build a noble State,
    Greater than Attica of yore.

Will any lift the ruthless hand;
    By any will that stroke be given,
Shall drive me from this beauteous land?—
    He drives me back for aye to Heaven!

No, lovely being! much I pray
That none may banish thee away;
For well I know how man is blest
Whilst thou continuest his guest.

I would, O Liberty, that he
Might bow to earth and worship thee;
I would thy temples here might rise
On marble columns to the skies;
I would have thee adored as one
Next to Jehovah and his Son.
Young men and maidens, let us raise
To her a daily hymn of praise!
Des Moines, upon thy verdant shore
May she continue evermore!
May never gaze on thee, that thing—
The curse of human-kind—a king;
May never look upon thy wave,
While time shall last, a trembling slave!
Upon thy northern wave the Sioux
Is paddling still his birch canoe.
What lovely prospect meets my view!—
The rolling prairies, like a sea
In vast and wild sublimity,
There lie with an unbroken sod,
Untilled but by the hand of God:
He sows the seeds of grass and flowers;
He moistens them with vernal showers.
But look abroad in summer-time;
I'm sure in England's foggy clime,
With all the aid that Art effords,
With all the efforts of rich lords,
A garden blooming half so fair
Never yet has flourished there.

What are her parks, to one who here
Has chased the bison, elk, and deer,
O'er pathless plains, and through wild woods,
And wandered in those solitudes,
Where could be heard no grating sound
Of mill, nor cattle lowing round,
Nor crowing cock, nor yelping hound,
Nor sportman's gun, nor tolling bell,
The charms of Nature to dispel,—
Has watched the beaver build like men,
And killed the wild duck aud marsh hen;
Caught wolves and badgers, lynx, raccoon,
And shot on Spirit Lake the loon?
Ah, Spirit Lake! she is to-day
As beautiful as Loch-Achray!
'T is true, the "Minstrel" here can view
No lofty rocks, no Ben-venue:
Here Nature doffs her awful charms;—
Holds out to him her lovely arms,
I mount on Fancy's wings the air;
I seek a woody island, where
Upon a grassy couch reclined,
Fond recollections throng my mind,
Of happy days, when but a child,
I glided o'er such waters wild,
And, glad, on every danger smiled.
The little boat my father guides;
My playful hands hang o'er its sides,
And dabble in the foaming waves,
That rise like spectres from the graves,—

I do not know their rage to fear;
Their music joyfully strikes mine ear
'Tis thus I yet on life's waves ride,
By no wild breakers terrified;
I let them roll unheeded by,
Nor seem to know the danger nigh,—
Content and hope fill up my breast;
And threat what will, I still am blest!
Protected by a Father's care,
Approach not fear; away despair!
The raging winds have sought their caves,
And now subsided are the waves;
Not e'en a rush is seen to shake;
So smoothe the surface of the lake,
I see the fishes at their play;
I see them quickly dart away.
What dreadful form to them appears,
That now so mightily wakes their fears?—
A giant monster moving slow,
And dips two frightful fins below.
Thus men take fright ofttimes as great
At monsters their own fears create;
Church-yards by night swarm with grim
   ghosts,
Dark Hades has dire fiends by hosts,
And Pluto reigns supreme o'er all
That dwell within the horrid wall.
We now pass round a point of land
Where branching cedars thickly stand;
Wild berries, plums, and grapes abound.

And nuts of many kinds are found.
But what a lovely prospect lies
Outspread before my gladdened eyes!
The lake with boats is dotted o'er
From yon small village on the shore;
The fisherman sinks down his seine
And rows toward that shore again;
And the light anchors others weigh
Who have been angling all the day,
And homeward turn, because the sun
His daily course has well-nigh run;
While each loud sound the paddles make
Is borne by Echo o'er the lake,
And her sweet voice is plainly heard
To answer each loud-spoken word.
But hark! what tender sound I hear,
That strikes so mournfully mine ear!
'Tis borne on Zephyr's wings from far,—
The music of a soft guitar.

ADIEU.

I love my contry's maidens,
   Wherever I may roam;
But those that are most dear to me
   Are of my village home;

Because I love that village;
   I love her hills around;
Her woods and her wild prairies;
   Her streamlets' murmuring sound.

There comes a voice unbidden,
　Nor can I tell thee why,
Commanding me to love my home,—
　That voice is from on high.

While I have been a stranger,
　Far from that home away,
There never has unkindness yet
　Beclouded my fair day.

No maid has e'er despised me,
　Although of high degree;
Nor has she ever spurned me
　From her sweet company.

Must the tear of bitter grief
　Now first be made to start;
Must the heaviest stroke be given
　Against my feeling heart,

By those I prize so highly
　Of my own village home,
By those I prize more highly far
　Than wealth or ancient Rome?

But now I am determined,
　Ah! never more to feel
Such cruel wound upon my heart,
　Worse than a wound of steel!

So, in the happy woods I'll seat
　Me on a mossy stone;

IOWA.

I'll strike upon my sounding harp
    And leave the maids alone!

Dame Nature, I shall woo her
    With all my words of love ;
I'll woo the flowers of the ground
    I'll woo the birds above ;

I'll woo the gentle sunset ;
    I'll woo the evening breeze,
While it sings on joyful wings
    Among my forest trees!

A large and handsome boat I see ;
It bears a happy company,
That came to spend a joyful day
Upon this little cape in play,—
Gathering fruits, and wreathing flowers;
Reclining 'neath the shady bowers
Formed by Nature's sylvan fingers,
Where, a wood-nymph, still she lingers,
Plucking warer-lilies fair,
To adorn her raven hair ;
Holding in her lovely hand
A branch of cedar for a wand;
Protecting all the living things
That walk the earth, or fly on wings ;
Directing the industrious bees
To take for mansions her tall trees;
Painting the wings of butterflies
With colors like the evening skies.

To-day, beneath her shades so cool,
Those of a Christian Sabbath-school
Sat down and drank of happiness,—
Drank from the cup of social bliss ;
But now at evening they forsake
The grove and sail upon the lake.
As towards their homes they haste along,
All are joined in sacred song.

A PSALM OF DAVID.*

Oh, now let us sing to the Lord a new song,
  For marvelous deeds hath He done ;
With His holy arm and right hand ever strong
  He hath the great victory won.

By love hath He conquered, salvation made
      known.
  And now may the heathen rejoice,—
To them is His righteousness openly shown ;
  They hear His kind welcoming voice.

How well He remembered in mercy and truth
  To smile upon Israel, too ;
The ends of the earth,—all the aged and youth—
  Are led His salvation to view.

Let all the wide world to Him joyfully raise
  A noise of thanksgiving on high ;
With the voice of a psalm on the harp, sing His
      praise,—
  Sing praise unto Him who is nigh.

                    * Psalm xcviii.

With trumpets and sound of the glad cornet make
A joyful noise to our King;
Let seas loudly roar, and their creatures awake,
And the world, and all in it, sing.

Let floods clap their hands; let the gladsome
    hills smile
Before Him who bade them have birth;
He cometh, and they shall behold Him erewhile
With righteousness judging the earth!

But now I leave this lake's wild shore,
Perhaps to visit it no more.
Iowa —thirteen years a State, *
And now appears among the great!
Let her proud banner be unfurled
And borne in triumph round the world!
"Oh, I have found the beauteous one,—
The fairest land beneath the sun!"
Thus strangers, when they first behold
This land more bright than glittering gold;
Thus speak they when their eyes first greet
Her plains, like boundless fields of wheat;
When first her dark green forests rise
Conspicuous before their eyes;
When first they see her rivers roll
Through fields exhaustless of rich coal;
When first her marble beds appear;
When to her lime-stone quarries near;
When they her mines of led explore;

* Admitted into the Union Dec. 28, 1846.

When they behold her iron ore
And copper on the river shore,
And fire-clay and quartzite sand,
And gypsum underneath the land.
Thus is she great in mineral worth;
She is the garden of the earth!
How very wise in all her laws!
How glorius in Freedom's cause!
On the Escutcheon give her far
The broadest stripe, the brightest star!
Escutcheon of the thirty-three,—
The coat-of-arms of Liberty,
And of a noble family!
Yes, Iowa indeed is fair;
Of streams of water has her share;
Is rich in minerals, and her soil
Will bless for aye the plowman's toil.
Who o'er the prairies looks abroad,
And does not see the hand of God
Preparing them through ages past
To be the homes of men who cast
The seed abroad, and reap again
A rich reward in golden grain!
Who has prophetic ken to tell
How many million here may dwell;
What mighty deeds will here be done;
What wreaths of laurel here be won!
What men appear whose names shall stand
An honor to their native land!

SAYLOR'S GROVE, JUNE, 1859.

IOWA.

PART THIRD.

(1882.)

Many changes have taken place since the spring of 1859. It is winter now of 1881-2. The urgent needs of a large family compel the author o accept gratefully the humble place of teacher of a country school, three miles from his rural cabin home. But his path lies along the beautiful Des Moines, all the way through thick woods a pleasant path indeed. He has reached the age of forty-four, perfect in health not having been seriously ill even one day in seventeen years. Why not now write his master-piece? Filled with this glorious hope, confident of the ripeness of his mind, the task is begun, and IOWA, PART THIRD is composed by the author while journeying, mornings and evenings to and from his little school.

IOWA.

PART THIRD.

——0——

THE FUTURE.

A MORNING'S MEDITATION ON THE BANKS OF THE DES
MOINES.

"Still true to reason be my plan." —AKENSIDE.

At forty-four with heart as young
As when a beardless boy I sung,—
At forty-four with hope the same
And love of honorable fame—
The same unconquered mind and free,
But chastened by Adversity—
O may the path that I have trod
Be hailed the narrow way to God!
At forty-four I strike anew
The harp laid down at twenty-two,—
Awake the patriotic strain
To rise into a grand refrain
Resounding over land and main—
A Hymn of Freedom bold and strong
The bane of Tyranny and Wrong.

Thy waves, Des Moines, thou happy Stream,
Emblem of life of virtue seem,
Gliding onward day and night,
Limpid, joyous, pure and bright.
The prince of Evil from below
Cannot retard the onward flow
Of God's great wave that has set in,
Submerging continents of sin.
The race of kings, like Pharao's host
Beneath that tidal wave is lost,
And grasping Greed and Avarice drown
And War and Poverty go down ;
But Love, Equality and Peace
Shall bless for aye the human race.
True Christianity restored,
Mammon no longer is adored—
All in one common brotherhood,
The good of all the greatest good—
Self-abnegation is the leaven
To metamorphose Hell to Heaven,
Transform this world of selfishness
Into a Paradise of bliss,
A Christian community—
Declaim against it Pharisee!
'Twas Selfishness deprived of life
Both Ananias and his wife—
It is the same to-day as then
(I speak as unto Christian men)
'Tis Selfishness keeps back a part—
Why, why conceive it in thy heart

To lie unto the Holy Ghost?
Thus life, O selfish soul, is lost!
No life has he who lives for pelf; .
No life has he who worships Self—
Immortal life is his who dies
For other's good a sacrifice—
While duty is a sacred word,
While to dishonor death's preferred,
While country, home and flag are dear,
While dims an eye the patriot's tear,
Thou'lt be remembered, Kinsman.
Of Iowa's twenty thousand braves
That rest in honored patriots' graves,
None had a larger heart that thine;
While Iowa's glorious sun shall shine
Thou'lt be remembered, Kinsman.
And Oh, I see the time quite near
When Selfishness shall disappear!
When each shall live and act as though
He were unto himself a foe—
So great his philanthropic zeal,
So wedded to the Commonweal,
As Kinsman gave his life, his all,
Responsive to his country's call,
So ever has Divinity
Incarnate in Humanity,
'Mid scenes of suffering and sin,
Displayed its heavenly origin.
The "better nature" will control,

5

In time at hand, the human soul,
The lion with the lamb shall dwell,
As old time prophesies foretell.
The darkest hour (so sages say)
Is just before the dawn of day;
Before the Negroe's shackles fell,
Gross darkness and the rebel yell!
Now intense darkness shades our eyes
Veiling the planetary skies—
The few grow rich the many poor
And tramps are dogged from every door
The millionaire would have his word
And e'en his very whisper heard,
And Congress bow before his nod
And Presidents cry "Gould is God!"
It cannot last; it must not stand;
No autocrat shall rule this land;
He would as well attempt to force
The Mississippi from her course.
The Freedom that the Fathers sought
Is pillowed on the common thought
And rests secure as Warren's fame
And Washington's immortal name:
The world will not have long to wait—
Hear Iowa greet a sister State:

IOWA TO CALIFORNIA—AN ODE OF 1878.

O'er sovereign States
    The slimy things—

Huge railroad rings
And syndicates—
　　Reign cruel kings.
　　　　Hail, California!

Toilers, dethrone
　　Those ghouls of greed!
　　It is decreed
That ye alone
　　Are kings indeed.
　　　　Hail, California!

O'er work, well done
　　Rejoice O State ;
　　Exult elate—
Swing glad upon
　　Thy golden gate !
　　　　Hail, California!

They spurn the yoke
　　Who plow and plod ;
　　They give the nod—
Thy people spoke
　　The voice of God !
　　　　Hail, California!

Now cheer on cheer !
　　Green, green's thy tree
　　Of Liberty,
And God is near

To aid the free !
Hail, California !

Not long will blindness hide from view
The rights of all and shield the few—
Not long the people now betrayed
Will bide the bonded debt unpaid ;
While billions from the toilers rung,
Are to the ravenous usurers flung.
What agent moves with mightier force
Than lightning in its downward course?
Almighty thought divinely wrought—
Invincible immortal thought !
The subtilest agent God has given ;
The grain of mustard seed, the leaven,
The Kingdom of the Christ from Heaven.
Say what you will, talk as you may,
We see the dawning of the day—
The day that sets all labor free
Establishing Equality ;
For labor now lfts up her head
As if awakened from the dead,
And her edict has gone forth
Over all the mundane earth :

THE EDICT OF LABOR.

Let the laws no longer say
"You must work and he may play"
What my own hard hands produce

Shall be sacred to my use;
The sweat of thine own face (as said
In Holy Writ) shall give thee bread,
But the helpless must be fed;
The aged and the little ones
Asking bread must not get stones
Ah, never call it "charity,"
The bread that is theirs rightfully—
Rightfully 'tis theirs to live;
Rightfully 'tis ours to give
Millions to support the poor—
Not a cent for tribute more—
Tribute to monopoly
And accursed Usury.
All the bounteous gifts bestowed
By the gracious hand of God,
Gifts like water, land and air,
All mankind may equal share;
That which Toil does not create
Is too all men consecrate:
No one may monopolize
The manna given from the skies;
All that God in kindness gives
Belongs to each alike that lives—
Let the laws no longer say:
"You must work and he may play."

Soon the battle will begin
Gainst the giant powers of Sin;
See the cause of God succeed!

Righteousness will conquer Greed ;
Private wealth will be unknown
In the day that hastens on—
Private capital no more
Shall enslave the toling poor ;
All the land will then be tilled
By the owners of the field ;
Their own hands will plow and sow ;
Their own hands will reap and mow—
Soon will perish Tenantry ;
Rent will die with Usury ;
Soon each man a home shall have ;
On his own proud acre live ;
Soon in cities (Sin's retreats)
Grass will grow upon the streets ;
Where now millionaires reside
There will owls securely hide ;
And the serpent and the toad
There will find a fit abode.
No longer will palatial domes
Look proudly down on humbler homes—
Every patriot will disdain
To dwell above the common plane—
The fundamental law shall be:
"Love, Peace and Uniformity."
The greatest—the most truly blest—
Will be the servant of the rest—
The Godlike man whose noble mind
Reaches farthest toward his kind—

IOWA.

The father of the fatherless ;
The widow's helper in distress.

Mark the working of the bee,
Fittest type of Industry,
How according to fixed plan
(Learn a lesson here, O man!)
Does she build her waxen cell,
And she builds the structure well.
Now is Nature's lesson taught
In the works the bee has wrought;
Thus within the human hive,
All alike may build and thrive—
None be rich and none be poor ;
All partakers of the store—
Each his part assigned to do;
Each to Nature's laws as true—
Institution will bring forth
Eden of the Fertile earth—
Justice will be brought about
When the drones are driven out.

Put your hands together, then;
Think and act, O working men !
Think what great Lycurgus did
For Sparta in an age of blood;
Remember, too, our patriots dead
And all they bravely did and said;
The glorious charter that they won —
The deed drawn up by Jefferson

Proclaiming man's equality
A promise of what was to be—
What was to be but is not yet,
A sun to rise and never set
When man shall find his highest good
And cease to shed his brothers' blood
And build a state that will eclipse
The promise of the Apocalypse.
For what they nobly did and said
Give honor to the patriot dead.

A HYMN TO THE DEAD.

We see the dead; we know them—touch their
    hands;
  While they enfold us in their loving arms—
Obey their voices; list to their commands—
  It is their fire our freezing bodies warms—
'Tis theirs all that we have, whatever stands,
  Endures, is valued, benefits or charms,
The dead bestowed upon us in their lives:
Lay earth to earth, what is it still survives?

The good that they have done—this, this is ours:
  It stands eternal and will not fall down—
But name the good they've done—built Babel
    towers?
  Acquired on fields of blood, the conquerors
    crown?

Wrenched states from states and added powers to
    powers?
  And filled the world with woe and their re-
    nown?
Not so, not so—a grander work they did,
More lasting than the firmest Pyramid.

Ah, to the dead we owe all that we have!
    Our institutions and inventions all—
Without their work none would be living save
    The acorn-eating savages. The wall
Betwixt the living and the dead—the grave—
    Hides nothing from us that we would recall—
The living are afar—the dead are near;
The living are unseen; the dead appear.

All that have fallen for their country's sake—
    They stand before us in our glorious laws—
The saints that graced the scaffold and the stake
    They live immortal in the people's cause;
'Tis only by the self-sacrifice we break
    The powers of evil and win God's applause—
His workers toil and suffer and expire;
And they alone are bidden: "Come up higher."

    Lo! future Iowa we see,
    The ripened fruit upon the tree
    Planted by the Deity.
    Mightily the tree has grown

In the countless ages gone ;
Its blossoms—what a grand array
Have opened in this later day!
Sure promise of a bounteous store,
Of luscious fruit forevermore.
At Wilson's Creek, Iowa made
Herself a name that cannot fade;
And her undaunted bravery won
To Union flag Fort Donelson
On Shiloh's mournful field she stood,
Her garments soaked with her own blood,
Her bravest sons in hundreds fall
By shot and shell and minnie ball;
At Corinth and Iuka hear
From Iowa boys the victor's cheer;
Port Gibson, Raymond, Champion Hill,
Black River Bridge, and grander still,
Above the clouds with Hooker, caught
Foretaste of glory as they fought!
But, oh, the fratricidal strife,
Where brother seeks a brother's life !
Let, let me not be understood
To claim that war can be a good.
It is unmitigated sin;
Nor are they conquerors who win ;
It is a serpent, (poets write),
That perishes of its own bite ;
('T is taught us in the Sacred Word,
Thy perish thus that take the sword;)
Yet men display on fields of war

The qualities that in them are,—
Exalted bravery, fortitude,
Self-sacrifice for other's good,—
· And in these qualities we see
Sure promise of what is to be,
When love shall rule and man be free.

THE PROMISE.

In halls where Peace rejoiced,
Voiced
By happy swains,
In sweet refrains,
And golden strains,
Bombs burst!

In halls,—places of prayer,
Where,
Devoutly heard
Was the Word
Of the Lord,
Bombs burst!

Lo! "Wars shall be no more!"
O'er
Seas of tears,
Through countless years
Faith's star appears!
Bombs burst!

Now Love and Progress speak,—
   Shriek:—
" The time is near
When human ear
Shall cease to hear
   Bombs burst!"

Peace would have smiled in '61,
Had but the people's will been done;
Yes, had their voice been fairly heard,
Rust would have gnawed the hateful sword;
But demon Madness ruled the hour
Begot of Greed and Lust of Power.
It was the few of shameless cheek,—
Base robbers of the poor and weak,—
That they might count their chattel slaves,
Forced millions to untimely graves.
The Muse of History will write:—
" *The rich man's war, the poor man's fight!*"
Be it proclaimed and understood,
War never seeks the people's good!
Her baneful name let them abhor;
All slavery is a state of war;
For tyranny's sustained by force;
Proclaim it, *War's the giant curse!*
With soldiery all Europe swarms,—
Four million sons of toil in arms!
O sons of toil, unite! unite!
Throw down your arms, and cease to fight!
What helpless and what hopeless things

Without you, are the race of kings !
But hark! a song of triumph hear,—
Its joyful accents ring out clear;
'T is Labor voices now a cry
That mounts exultant to the sky.

A SONG OF LABOR.

Labor will triumph, boys—no one can doubt it,
    men ;
  We are all brothers, we children of toil—
We will be slaves no more ; loud let us shout it,
    then;
  But will be freemen, we sons of the soil !
    All will be joy and peace ;
    Wars and oppressions cease,
Since we will butcher our brother no more—
    Now every wound we stanch ;
    Hold out the olive branch
To every toiler upon every shore!

Labor makes all the guns; Labor must handle
    them ;
  Labor mans all the ships on the high seas ;
Why do we fight for kings? Why do we dandle
    them
  Like mewling babies upon our rough knees?
    How will the kings and lords
    Manage the guns and swords

When the hard-handed, the ninety-and-nine
    All of us break our ranks,
    Bowing the kings our thanks
Shout back: "We, guns, drums and banners
      resign!

The world a republic, boys! Grandly united
    men;
    The millions are guided by love and not hate—
They dwell in the sunshine of peace all delighted,
    then;
      No poor and no rich and the meek are the
        great!
      Brothers and working men,
      Give us your hands again!
Now we are happy and ever shall be:—
    On to the Rhine! We say
    Prune now the vine we may;
We plant and we dwell 'neath our vine and fig
    tree!

The land is the people's, boys! Railroads and
    telegraphs;—
    Giant Monopoly yields up the ghost!
See old king Gold is dead! loudly the toiler
    laughs!
    Who now by labor will save up the most?
    Dead is king Alcohol
    Poverty, crime and all—
No use for gibbets for jails or police—

Here is fair play, my boys;
Shout it and make a noise;
Labor has triumphed and man is at peace!

But patriots all be on your guard;
One kind of devils go out hard—
And Greed and Tyranny and War
Among this kind of devils are.
The framers of our written law
The danger to our peace foresaw;
And early made provision strong
To guard against the threatened wrong
Declared in language grandly plain
That standing armies are our bane.
They gnaw upon the nation's health;
They bite and tear the Commonwealth.
Despite of all our fathers said
The serpent raises high its head;
An army is equipped and paid
And "soldiering" becomes a trade.
"Militia" of our fathers' plan
Counts every able-bodied man;
The people learned the use of arms
To guard their families and farms;
For treacherous Indians blind to law
Filled peaceful settlements with awe—
While we've the ballot and the sword
Whose word is law? The people's word!
But why have we arrayed to-day
A host of soldiers under pay?

Why do we now so violate
The Constitution of our State?
When these have power to overawe
The people then the Sword is law!
The "enemy hath scattered tares"
Who for pretention makes long prayers—
But who is he? The millionaires!
So ravenous for wealth and power
E'en "widow's houses they devour."
These ghouls let all just men contemn
As scorned by Christ of Bethlehem!
The gnilty lay awake all night
Quaking with terror and affright;
Just so these heartless robbers quake
Fearing the people may awake
To right their wrongs and vengance take:
Therefore they frame a tyrant law
To keep the "dangerous class" in awe—
Framed with a deep and dark design
For one to rule the ninety-nine.
The master formerly was " lash "—
Who would be master now? King " Cash !"
This king now speaks and says :—

                    " My will
Is that the people shall not drill!
Place 'Constitution' on the shelf,
Lest Labor—wronged—protect herself,
A sleek, select, 'Prætorian Band'
Shall be the guardians of the land,

To put down strikes, and charge and kill
The starving working men, at will;
Because 'tis clear, the laboring mass
Is now become a 'dangerous class,'
As were the blacks when old John Brown
At Harper's Ferry won renown,—
Had these been armed, 'tis plain, the yoke
Of slavery at once they'd broke,—
We must have troops held under pay
To keep the laboring class at bay."
Plain words are these--their meaning clear—
May every freeman hark and hear!
Above the people now behold
A class most insolent and bold:
See Legislatures, bought and sold!
The railroad magnate spreads his tent
Right in our halls of government;
The banking Syndicate a God—
He shakes his locks and gives the nod—
From Saratoga thunders forth
His mandates to the mundane earth—
The mass asleep; their rights the sport
Of Congress, President and Court
So venal as would put to shame
E'en Arnold of unhappy fame!
Why, why asleep? The cruel strife
Had almost quenched the nation's life;
And who can wonder, at its close
If tired Nature sought repose?
Reaction follows action sure

6

In all we do and all endure:
Now slimy reptiles noiseless creep
And bleed their victim in his sleep—
But hark! Who speaks the warning word?
Oh be the Patriot's warning heard!

THE PATRIOT'S WARNING.

Beware, beware
The millionaire!
He "all in all," puffed up with pride—
The Constitution and the laws
See, see him bound to override
Making no pause!

Beware, beware!
The millionaire
With tyrant hand struck Freedom down
In her first home, in her first home!
She sank and left but the renown
Of Greece and Rome!

Beware, beware
The millionaire!
A deadly foe, a deadly foe
To thee, O working man, to thee
Will pause not till he overthrow
Our Liberty!

Beware, beware
The millionaire!
Ah, one by one our rights are blown

Blown to the wind, blown to the wind—
Philistines fill the Judges' throne,
  And Samson blind!

'Tis not the form that we commend
Of government—but 'tis its end:
If it be dubbed "democracy"
And fosters aristocracy
What is it but black tyranny?
If't looks to "payments" and to "rents"
'Tis hatefullest of governments—
If't seeks to build up happy homes
Men cry with joy: "The Savior comes!
This is the New Jerusalem—
Our King is Christ of Bethlehem!"
Who dare invade the hallowed dome
That holy place, the humblest home?
Who desecrate the sacred place?
The holiest of holies who deface?
Pull down the home—the straw-thatched
      shed
More sacred than the tombs of the dead?
Of tyranny beware, beware;
He has no heart, the millionaire!

Four million chattel slaves released
Their cry of agony has ceased—
It was a struggle that the men
Who saw it would not see again—
A victory for Labor won;
But still the conflict must go on;

Eternal vigilance will be
Ever the price of liberty;
For freedom is not adamant,
But only a most tender plant
That must be kept with watchful care
Lest blight destroy or wintry air.
Much has been done, much is to do
Before the promised land we view—
Every form of cruelty
Is a form of tyranny—
End cruelty of every form
And Tyranny you thus disarm.
When we have reached the true confine
Of freedom we hold man divine;
Then prisons change their rigid rules
And are converted into schools;
The gallows (that most foul disgrace
Of nations and the human race)
Will pass away as has the cross
And no one ever mourn its loss.
The aim of human law has been
To kill the sinner, not the sin;
He that no sin has ever known
May at the sinner cast a stone;
The ninety-nine upon safe ground
Seek for the one lost sheep till found
And when 'tis found gladly restore
The wanderer to the fold once more—
John Howard and Eliz'beth Fry
We hold in grateful memory—

The poison of the soul remove
By surest antidote—by love;
'Tis love will melt the hardest heart
And force foul demons to depart—
Lift up the fallen one—restore
Her to an upright walk once more;
The magic power of love is seen—
Rejoice O Mary Magdalene!
Ten thousand doors now open wide
To bring thee to the Saviour's side;
Thousands of thousands seek thy good
The universal sisterhood—
Mankind a true fraternity,
Humanity one family,
Benighted one, abandon thee!
No never, while still glows the gem
Of night, the Star of Bethlehem;
No never, while the Sun divine
Of Righteousness our day shall shine,
O Son of God and Son of Man!
No inspiration's higher than
Thy life! Immortal Energy,
Invincible as Deity!
Unfolding lovely leaf and bloom,
Enshrined in emblematic tomb:—
The leaf of hope, the bloom of love,
Graft from the Tree of Life above.
No written message didst thou pen,
But emphasized one word to men—
Thy life the emphasis; the word

(Above the written one preferred,)
The word is "Love," which prophets saw
Dethrone ('fulfill') the bloody "Law;"
Now, only thy command remains,
(It all the written law contains,
Makes every man on earth our brother,)
Thy great command, "*Love one another!*"
Love brethren only, what reward?
He loves all men who loves the Lord.
Bright on the banner of our cause,
Read, "*Love engraven on the laws!*"
The Sermon on the Mount behold,
In letters brighter far than gold,
Made, by the people's stern command,
The "Constitution" of the land.
It must be written in our laws :
" No slavery for any cause!"
See convict slaves farmed out to Craig,
While their families starve or beg.
Pay then wages—fair return
For all they do and all they earn;
Deprived of liberty—confined—
They can no longer harm mankind ;
Now let us point them to the road
That leads to righteousness and God.

The cause of sin must be assigned
To wrong ideas in the mind—
Remove the wrong ideas and Saul
At once is transformed into Paul!—
But Cruelty cannot remove

The wrong ideas—only Love !
A physician for the sick;
Tender nursing for the weak..
Man never falls so low that he
May not arise to dignity—
An heir of God ; joint heir with Christ
Who for our sins was sacrificed.
Where lies the blame for all the crime
That so disgraces now our time ?
It rests upon society—
It rests upon community ;
Community owes every child
An education that will build
Into the edifice designed
The structure of the heart and mind;
"As bent the twig the tree's inclined."
Those slums of poverty and greed
(The pestilential cities) breed
Infection in the atmosphere
That grows more deadly year by year—
"Street Arabs" never out of sight—
Goods-boxes shelter them at night—
Misfortune's "Children in the Wood"
Dying of cold and want cf food;
Oh, gather in the little ones,
Nor feed them serpents and hard stones !
See now the Priest pass by in pride ;
The Levite on the other side—
Who is the tender-hearted man ?
Who is the good Samaritan ?

Say 'tis the State—the Commonwealth—
Shall give them food—restore their health;
Shall fold them in her sheltering arms;
Her roof protect from angry storms!
Time hurries by; these little ones
Grow up to be her stalwart sons;
Support her when her locks are gray—
Her love with gratitude repay!

The Old is dead!   Gladly we view
The rising glory of the New!
Now when Zone answers to Zone
By telegraph and telephone
And the Desert hears the scream
Of the moster belching steam,
It is a fact all must perceive—
Perceiving it all must believe:
The methods that bore fruit of yore
Will blossom in this world no more.
A ukase Progress has decreed
From which mankind cannot recede,
That:

            "In an age when Church and State
Are wide divorced and separate,
The State must not attempt to shirk,
But carry on the mighty work
The Church so worthily began
To mitigate the woes of man."
The "Sisters"—none but thee, good **Lord,**
Can give them adequate reward!

The foundling's and the orphan's shield;
The soldier's bleeding from the field.

Old means no longer adequate,
It has devolved upon the State,
With "Charity" kept out of sight
To give the helpless "natural right."
Man's natural rights! With pointed dart
Engrave it on the hardest heart,
And every freeman, too, give ear
And he that is the deafest hear:
If law and justice were the same,
Then law could have no other aim
Than to enforce these rights and give
Their benefits to all that live;
And when so done, as God designed
The State becomes "eyes to the blind,
Feet to the lame"—the helpless all
Upon her as a mother call—
Are by her fondled and caressed
As infants nourished at the breast.
To criminals are given, too,
The right of reclamation due:
The State is arbiter of both
Their mental and their moral growth.
All pains and penalties have failed
Since Jesus to the cross was nailed—
Failed signally. The end designed
They never reach—the victim's mind;
Nor can the point be put too strong

That pains and penalties are wrong.
Can we by freezing soften wax?
Or split the ocean with an axe?
Pains even of the least degree,
Proclaim existing Tyranny ;
And fines are only robbery :
A sot before the Court is led
And fined—his children cry for bread ;
The law can break the drunkard's cup
And thus can make him give it up—
Destroy the rattlesnake and then
'Twill surely never bite again !
What devil, Christian England, say,
Has drugged, with opium, Cathay ?
Put down the trade! Oh, burning shame !
Out, damned spot upon thy name !—
Pile opium in heaps around
And opium eaters will abound ;
While alcohol in rivers runs,
Columbia mourns her perished sons !
O Alcohol ! Thou demon fell
As ever left the court of Hell !
May all the Wrath and Hate and Scorn,
That ever were conceived and born,
Be armed against thy hateful life
With sharpened spear and poison knife,
And may thy cruel heart soon feel
The vengeful bite of hungry steel !
But woman ! When thy voice is heard
The fiend will vanish at a word—

It will be heard ! At thy command
See now the demon quit the land !
And e'en the army's guns and noise
Are silenced by thy gentle voice :
Not in tempest, not in flame,
Not in earthquake ; but there came
To Horeb where Elijah stood
"A still small voice"—the voice of God !

But lo ! the sun is risen high
And shines resplendent in mid sky—
Thy Poet's blessing with thee dwell,
O lovely Stream ! and now farewell !

Hunter's Ridge December, 1881.

LINES.

God is our only King;
   Let us in gladness sing,—
Shout on the land and sea
   Union and Liberty!

We will deal justly, then,
   As becomes noble men ;
Shout on the land and sea
   Union and Charity.

God is our only King;
   Let us His praises sing,—
Shout on the land and sea
   Union and Victory.

POEMS
OF THE PRESENT.

(1882-3.)

Whatever is personal in the following pieces is aimed only at public men, "makers of history" (as the assassins of Cavendish and Burke in Ireland, styled themselves.) A great master of English song has said: "A poet is justified in writing against a particular person when that person becomes a public nuisance." Can there be a greater "public nuisance" than is the hired assassin of his country's liberty?— than is the venal attorney who for a fee becomes the procurator of Satan on earth, bribed to attempt the defeat of the establishment of Christ's kingdom of temperance sobriety, and righteousness amongst men?

It is customary with many of our American poets to go to foreign lands for themes. Two of the following pieces have reference to the war in Egypt; but to-day, the world is brought so nearly under one roof that wars are no longer of merely local interest. The themes chosen by the author afford him an opportunity of giving expression to his deep abhorrence of war and to the confident hope of a better future for mankind. We are in the dawn of a new era of civilization—the long-promised reign of the "Prince of Peace;" and blessed is he (or she) who helps on its inauguration; and thrice blessed the poet who shall sing acceptably that golden period. His is the song of the angels: Peace on Earth; good will to men." With him partizanship is lost in patriotism and sectarianism in the religion of Jesus: "love to God and love to man."

THE OUTLOOK.

———o———

PART THE FIRST.

THE COMING REFORM.

OPTIMIST, PESSIMIST.

"The Earth hath he given to the children of men.'
—DAVID.

OPTIMIST.

Good morning, neighbor Pessimist ; why do you
     look so sour?
Good news I bring you: soon will end accursed
     kingly power;
And wars no more will scourge the world; but
     blest Equality
Will wed the lovely angel Peace; and we shall
     live to see
God's Kingdom set up in the earth; the promis-
     ed Shiloh come,
And Poverty shall disappear. The glad millen-
     nium
Will rise upon us bright as noon before you are
     aware ;
Then cast aside your gloomy looks and trample
     on Despair!

Pessimist.

The end of kings, kind Optimist, we never shall
　　behold ;
Proud tyrants bind us now in chains—king Al-
　　cohol, king Gold.
The first is Satan loosed on earth to reign a thou-
　　sand years ;
The beast of the Apocalypse, the second king
　　appears.
These war against the sons of men; resistless
　　is their power;
The authors of all wretchedness ; the helpless
　　they devour—
No promise yet of better things; the world grows
　　worse each year;
A night of gloom the future shows ; no gleams of
　　morn appear ;
But rather darkness visible—a blackness unde-
　　fined
Obscures the hope of good to man—gross dark-
　　ness clouds his mind.
The people are a race of fools—a flock of owls
　　and bats :
Their wisdom is a sham, how blind, a herd of
　　hungry rats !
The "piper pipes," the multitude rush madly
　　through the town,
Till in the the sea they are engulfed—behold the
　　vermin drown !

A glass of beer will buy their vote; the statesman, for a "pass,"
Will be to Gould or Vanderbilt a most devoted
ass.
A mess of pottage gains the best; their birth-right
they resign;
Thus avarice drives the people mad, as devils
drove the swine.
We live to see the end of wars; see blest Equality!
Behold all Christendom in arms! An aristocracy
Has grown here in a score of years, and mush-
room millionaires
Now seize the reins of sovereignty. The patriot
despairs!
'Tis plausible to look for good? No; "facts are
stubborn things,"
Can hope wipe out the race of Knaves and break
dishonest "rings"?
God's Kingdom is a crazy dream, yet let him
dream who will!
Such dreams are sweet, good Optimist: but truth's
a bitter pill!

OPTIMIST.

Methinks your mother nourished you, dear Pessimist, on gall;
Your bump of hope indeed is weak; your bump
of faith is small.

From savagery mankind have risen; 'twas Pro-
    gress led them forth
To triumph over matter and to conquer all the
    earth;
The mountains they have leveled down; the hills
    they have brought low,
The law is: "They shall conquer still, shall van-
    quish every foe."
The prophet saw the blessed day; saw blossom
    as the rose
The desert of the human mind; and we may well
    suppose
That he who tames the elements and yokes them
    to his cars,
Will tame his savage passions too, and put an
    end to wars,
The puny tribe of millionaires awhile may buzz
    and sting;
But, mark me, gloomy Pessimist, the people will
    be king!
The people are a mammoth strong, resistless
    when they move,
And progress is continuous as of the stars above:
No going back; but onward still—right onward
    in their course;
Yea on and on forever and omnipotent their
    force.
Most subtile are ideas, friend; though subtile
    they are strong!

Their fiat is: "Close up the gates gainst robbery
    and wrong."
King Alcohol must die the death ; king Gold
    must bow the knee ;
The hand that grasps the thunderbolt like Joves,
    will yet be free !
Man will be free ! Equality will come to bless
    the Earth,
And Poverty shall disappear and Freedom have
    new birth.

PESSIMIST

Did not great Rome succumb to gold? Corrup-
    tion rang her knell;
Her toilers robbed by millionaires, she tottered
    and she fell!
The Gracchi thought to stem the tide; their ef-
    forts were in vain ;
The tribunes of the people fell ; her patriots were
    slain.
The "rich man" struck the fatal blow ; accurst
    Monopoly
Destroyed the mighty Commonwealth and stran-
    gled Liberty.
The ' rich man" knows no law but greed, and
    governments are made
An engine of oppression dire, to tyranny an aid.
He robs by law ; the army fights to force the
    poor to yield

To him the substance of their toil, the products
    of the field,
Thus Ireland now is overrun with Red-coat sol-
    diery,
To force the slaves that till the lands again to bow
    the knee.
When force shall fail will fraud come in, assas-
    sinations, guile:
The rich will rule; the poor must serve now, on,.
    and all the while;
There is no hope for him who toils; relief will
    be denied;
His choice must lie 'twixt slavery and and death
    by suicide.

OPTIMIST.

I cannot say to you, my friend, that you are
    wholly right;
'Tis gloomy now I must admit; but day suc-
    ceeds the night.
The evils that cannot be borne will soon be
    thrown aside,
And then will rise the better day the prophets
    have descried—
That brighter day shall surely come when labor
    will combine
And walk together brothers all, the mighty-
    ninety nine—
The one—how feeble is his arm when stalwart
    Labor strikes;

The flood pours forth submerging all since
broken are the dykes—
The time's at hand when shall arise the flood of
working men,
And autocrats shall fly for life and thrones will
topple then :
We hear the mutterings of the storm ; the So-
cial Democrat,
The Nihilist, Trade's Union, all have issued their
fiat.
Upon a higher plane of love the people take their
stand;
The world is free ! King Gold is dead and La-
bor owns the land !
A bloodless revolution hail ! Green Ireland now
behold
Assume her former dignity, her prowess as of
old !
Her sons have shown their native worth; her
daughters have outdone
The heroines of history—unfading laurels won ;
The sword no longer will be sought to right the
toilers' wrongs ;
For peaceful means more potent are in breaking
Slavery's thongs.

PESSIMIST.

The toilers they are brutal dolts—a pack of
senseless curs !

Tobacco is their daily bread; their drink is swill.
  Yea, worse,
Their brains are cooked with alcohol; their bloat-
  ed stomachs burst—
They belch and vomit lager beer—of God they
  are accurst!
The people (I must speak the truth) deserve the
  blows they get;
Omnipotent you say they are, the drunken, brain-
  less set!
Like sheep they lick the bloody hand that grasps
  the fatal knife;
They bleat for salt—see mutton chops for Dives
  and his wife!
You boast of "progress" in the past; you augur
  progress still;
If it be progress, friend, alas! that progress is
  down hill!
Our fathers stood like men indeed; of them we
  justly brag;
They fought John Bull; what do we now; Salute
  the British flag!
Such is the "progress" we have made; such
  progress soon will bring
A House of Lords and Monarchy—long live Jay
  Gould, our king!
'Tis money rules! The people fall prostrate be-
  fore the throne;
Their bread is gone; the hungry curs now gladly
  gnaw a bone!

OPTIMIST.

The drunkards are a feeble folk ; besotted ones
   are few ;
The multitude are sober, man ! intemperance
   they eschew ;
Tobacco will be thrown aside, the time is very
   near
When woman by her gentle voice will end its
   vile career ;
But beer, wine, ale and alcohol will first go by
   the board ;
Then opium and tobacco she will banish with a
   word.
So take a happier view of things, my very worthy
   friend ;
Believe the time is near at hand when wrong
   shall surely end ;
And let us cherish gentle thoughts and let it be
   our plan
To build up human happiness and free race of
   man.
Another day, good Pessimist, we may again re-
   new
This very friendly dialogue, though now we say
   adieu.

May 8, 1882,

THE OUTLOOK.

——o——

PART THE SECOND.

THE TRIUMPH OF MONOPOLY.

OPTIMIST, PESSIMIST.

"The wicked shall not inhabit the earth."—Solomon.

OPTIMIST.

A happy New Year, Pessimist, how glad am I
    to see
The dawn of this auspicious year eighteen and
    eighty-three!
This year great changes will be wrought, greater
    than e'er before
Increasing human happiness and lifting up the
    poor,
Until Equality shall come to bless on every hand
And Peace and Love and Brotherhood prevail in
    every land.

PESSIMIST.

Facts, facts, sweet friend, hold fast to facts ; be-
    hold the dire event,

Reaction surely setting in. A "Stalwart" President

Arrayed against the common weal; and (crankiest of cranks)

He pettifogs for usurers and glorifies the banks;

Bewails the prosperous times we have and (shame on him!) regrets

That Uncle Sam so rapidly is paying off his debts!—

A little while ago we heard: "The Greenback (it does say it)

'United States will pay' so much well then why don't she pay it?

Pay off the Greenbacks," was the cry; "let this not be delayed;

They draw no interest; but the bonds, 'tis dangerous if they're paid

Repudiate? Not so indeed; the interest promptly pay—

The principal—Oh let that stand until the judgment day!"

OPTIMIST.

Who pleads for this? A patriot true that seeks his country's good!

A happy method of relief (by him so understood)

The burden of taxation rests too heavily just now

On those that moil: "who toil and spin" and
    those that hold the plow;
This will be lifted from their backs; and men of
    every trade
Will have more time to give to books and resting
    in the shade—
This, I opine, explains the wish the President
    expressed;
It is to give relief to toil and joy to every breast.

PESSIMIST.

Our President—with due respect I speak the
    honored word;
I give the office reverence due; but truth--let
    that be heard—
What interest does he seek to serve? the public
    interest? Nay!
Does he the multitude regard? the general voice
    obey?
He is the tool of syndicates—a servile sycophant
And hireling agent of John Bull, like office huck-
    ter Grant;
The "bosses" that he knuckles to, at Saratoga
    meet
Whenever kindly Autumn comes chasing the
    Summer's heat;
But who are they the Lords and Gods who rule
    our President

And who, to-day, *de facto*, are our boasted "Government"?
Our Congress sits to do their will; it bows before
their nod;
The Khedives of our subject State kneel down to
kiss the rod!
'Tis coward England holds us thus her tributary
slaves;
We scorn her armies; but her gold our road to
bondage paves.
The "burden of taxation" dire will be removed,
alas!
Not from the toilers' shoulders; but the greedy
banking class,
The agents of the Barings and the Rothchilds
who enthrall
This people, they will have their way and pay no
tax at all.
The scheme to "amend the tariff laws" is for this
purpose set,
To free the banks from taxes and prolong our
bonded debt.
Hark! what a hideous cry we hear of "surplus
revenue;"
While still the public debt remains, how wickedly
untrue!
But Lombard street's sole master here as well as
on the Nile,
And we, enchained by Usury, slaves to the "parent isle!"

Vile Usury! it wrings from us the products of
    our soil
And holds our farmers bound and gagged like
    Egypt's sons of toil;
The British Government (the lords, the aristoc-
    racy)
Has now in thrall our working men, rules our
    democracy;
Draws from us tribute far beyond the tribute she
    obtains
From all her Orient provinces and Africa in
    chains.

OPTIMIST.

You do not mean that we, to-day, (as Athens
    was of old)
Are sold by venal demagogues for bribes of for-
    eign gold!
That here democracy succumbs, betrayed by
    hungry curs,
Our liberties all sacrificed to lust of gold; and
    worse,
The multitude hoodwinked, seduced, bound down
    with iron chains
Because they lack the eyes to see; to know they
    lack the brains;
And England's grown so wise that she outflanks
    us in the fight

And, like the wily Woolsey, charges on us in
    the night,
Surprises us while fast asleep and drives us from
    our works,
Then makes us underlings and serfs, like Chris-
    tians are to Turks!
Who will believe the tale you tell? Who listen
    to you croak?
Your arguments are only bosh; your fire is only
    smoke!

PESSIMIST.

True, true indeed that Athens fell; fell Freedom's
    grand stronghold
And e'en Demosthenes himself took Alexander's
    gold;
The patriot brave whom Philip feared, bore home
    the golden bowl—
Prostrate her leaders, Athens drooped and Free-
    dom lost her soul!
How many a brave Demosthenes succumbs to
    bribery here!
How many a greedy demagogue grasped Credit
    Mobilier!
Decayed and rotten are the hearts of our great
    public men—
How many of the tried prove true? O say not
    one in ten!

One in ten thousand's far beyond the truth when
    truth is told;
Our blood-bought liberty is lost; bartered for
    British gold!
All public spirit, too, is dead; the Patriot is un-
    heard—
The printing press, what is it, say? The grave
    where Truth's interred;
And lying "matter" buys its place a hundred
    cents a line;
Thus "editorials" "patent sides" for usurers base-
    ly whine!
The Freedom of the press is lost; for giant Av-
    arice
Stands over it with club in hand; he rules the
    printing press.
He rules the courts (the specious plea of "public
    policy"
Conceals the bane of Freedom's life, the wolf,
    grim Tyranny.)
Monopoly is king to-day. The hateful " golden
    calf"
Guards all the avenues of thought; controls the
    telegraph—
Controls the bench, controls the church, and
    worse, controls the schools.
The people thus are hoodwinked, mocked, con-
    converted into fools.
Our poor men are our patriots; the patriot must
    be poor;

For all the "powers that be" to-day, they kick
    him from the door—
The door to preferment and bread, to all employ
    and place,
And public sentiment applauds while thieves spit
    in his face!
The ragged, hungry, homeless "tramp" is hated
    like a fiend;
Train robbers, rogues and miscreants by public
    voice are screened.
Who were the "tramps" that wandered forth
    millions in '78
Begging for crumbs from door to door and driv-
    en from State to State?
Resumption's victims—working men—the plun-
    dered, wronged, waylaid,
By act of Congress pauperized, thrown out of
    work, betrayed!
Resumption(ukase of John Bull) a thousand fath-
    oms deep
Above the lands of Uncle Sam, his cattle and
    his sheep,
A sea of mortgages it spread, and never, never-
    more
Our farmers and our workingmen will stand upon
    the shore;
But buried deep, a prey to "sharks"—devoured
    by British greed—
A twenty billion mortgage debt, that never ('tis
    decreed)

Shall be made less in principal, and all our sur-
  plus grain
And pork and beef, cotton and wool shrewd Eng-
  land will obtain
As interest on our " honest debt" that was upon
  us laid
By robber legislation, by a "money famine" raid,
Sorest famines!—born of law—contraction is the
  bane
Of all prosperity to toil; it empties every vein
And artery of the nation's life, and, wanting blood
  and breath,
Activity is lost to her, her quietude is death !
Her factories still, her workers tramps, impover-
  ished, begging bread,
Now toll the bells; bring out the hearse; Colum-
  bia is dead!
The ermined stab her to the heart; the Courts
  o'erthrow our laws,
The government is crushed betwixt an Alliga-
  tor's jaws !

OPTIMIST.

You ever see the darker side; Despair leads you
  astray.
Do harken to the voice of Hope that shows a
  brighter way!
These hopeful times! Most glorious times!
  change, change is in the air!

Mark the awakened public sense, awakened everywhere !

Immortal deeds will soon be done ; the banner is
unfurled

That will be borne triumphantly around a new-
saved world !

" Progress" inscribed upon its folds in letters large
and plain;

This is the day that was foretold for Christ to
come again !

His blessed presence is now felt and soon will all
mankind

Be close united by his Truth; be brethren of one
mind.

How weak, how frail, how impotent are all the
powers of Wrong!

How mighty is the cause of Right; the cause of
Truth, how strong!

Can British money-mongers hold the plunging
comet back ?

Can half a score of millionaires throw Progress
from the track ?

Close all the avenues of thought; shut out the
light of day?

No, we may speak by telephone and thought
will find a way

To penetrate the thickest gloom where Avarice
holds control

And shine a brilliant meteor in every human
    soul;
Yea truth will flame this very year a grand elec-
    tric light
That will abolish from the earth the very name
    of night.
Ah "no more night" "no need of sun," the hap-
    py day foretold;
New light now shines upon the world; the New
    supplants the Old
Our bonded debt will soon be paid; our farms
    will soon be freed
From mortgages—the mass will rise and strangle
    Giant Greed:
Columbia cannot be bound down in shackles
    very long;
She will arise in all her strength and throttle
    Giant Wrong!
She speaks—the judges on the bench are wise to
    heed her word;
But now you say they would attempt the role of
    George the Third.
There is but one thing courts may do; they have
    no other choice,
Their pathway is but this alone: *Echo the people's
    voice!*
Courts make our laws; courts change the text; a
    different meaning place
Upon the statute than designed; the genuine coin
    debase!

They might as well attempt to change the Missis-
  sippi's course;
To make her flow from south to north and speed
  back to her source—
America will have no King; the people are su-
  preme;
Their voice will be her law as long as flows that
  giant stream.
A Happy New Year then to you; to all on this
  wide earth—
Oh may this be the happiest year since hailed the
  Saviour's birth
With gladsome songs the heavenly choir—the
  glorious angel band—
Now peace to all and bread (aye, more) freedom
  to every land!

Jan. 14, 1883.

THE OUTLOOK.

——o——

THE TYRANTS OF THE GOWN.

OPTIMIST, PESSIMIST.

*"Servants have ruled over us.   *   *   *   The joy of our
heart is ceased; our dance is turned into mourning."*
JEREMIAH.

PESSIMIST.

Dead, dead and damned! just as I said; the er-
    mined stab our laws;
The fatal axe has come down hard upon the tem-
    perance cause—
Yea, "dead and damned" are modest terms to fit
    the woeful fate
To which their sovereignty is brought—the peo-
    ple's once so great;
But now the State is Lawyer Wrong; the peo-
    ple are the sport
Of railroad kings and whiskey rings that rule
    through him the court!

OPTIMIST.

Tush, tush! You magnify a mote; for Wrong
    his race has run
'Mongst any dozen barristers there's many a great-
    er one.

PESSIMIST.

Not so, not so; he now stands forth King of the
    Iowa bar
And e'en the judges on the bench beside him pig-
    mies are—
Pigmies forsooth! he placed them there; he gave
    them life and breath
And o'er them like a Roman sire holds power of
    life and death.
Those mewler (sucklings) on the bench (all honor
    to Judge Beck!)
Must knuckle down to Ex-Judge Wrong (a thief
    would save his neck!)
Because his power's increased of late, backed by
    the whiskey rings;
In caucuses omnipotent! Almighty! King of
    Kings!

OPTIMIST.

You certa'nly are mad, my friend; does not the
    genera' voice

Secure us judges? Worthy men raised by the
    common choice
To honored place, they guard our rights; depend-
    ent on our will
They as our tribunes must be true; our " royal law
    fulfill."

PESSIMIST.

Your theory is fair enough, and, as a theory, true;
But then it melts before the facts; in practice 'twill
    not do.
Crude, crude indeed the methods are by which
    the " people" rule;
The "bosses" are the government; show me a
    party tool—
Show me the king of caucuses; show me the hid-
    den " wires"
By which the party puppets dance and I will show
    you liars
That voice the party policy—and "policy" 's the
    word
That calls together party curs, rallys the " com-
    mon herd."
The people bow to " policy" and "policy" means
    " wrong,"
That wickedness shall rule the State; the weak
    shall rule the strong;
The many to the few succumb; manhood succumb
    to wealth

The millions to monopoly—thus fails the public
 health!

Do you assert that leadership (or "bossism," if
 you will)
Defeats the ends of government; stabs at its heart
 to kill?
Were not the leaders ("bosses") all consulted in
 the fight
Against the "Beast," King Alcohol, when Wrong
 succumbed to Right?
Was this great work an accident, and so the party
 Kings
Combine to quench our Samson's eyes and crop
 our eagle's wings?

The great result was woman's work, and, if it
 could have stood,
Would soon have grown a giant oak o'ershadow-
 ing all the wood—
A "Charter Oak" so grand, the world, ah, every
 human soul
Had cried ere long: "Give her a voice; let woman e'en control
The destinies of every land, give her the sovereign
 right
To speak by ballot, let her vote and thus dispel
 the night—

The gloomy, baleful night of crime, of vice, de-
    bauchery—
'Ring in the reign of Christ on earth,' the true
    Democracy!"
The lawyer's bull, lo! with his horns has gored
    the farmer's ox ;
This "woman's movement" must be quashed; it
    is not orthodox,
Suits not the purposes of those who hide behind
    the screen
And wield the potent party lash and manage the
    " machine"—
So 'tis o'erthrown, the woman's work, the tem-
    perance cause is dead ;
I nail this thesis to the door: " *Wrong knocked
    it on the head.*"
He saw that he could kill the maid; the Devil
    whispered "well;"
He raised his hand; he threw the dart; the beaute-
    ous damsel fell,
And now lies prostrate in her blood ; but he that
    did the deed
Will live to rue the sinful act; for " sovereign mercy"
    plead.
The history of every man is written, not with
    pen;
But on the living hearts and souls of his poor fel-
    low men ;
Rather a millstone to his neck and cast into the
    sea

Than add, through lust of gold, one grain to human misery,

OPTIMIST.

'Tis true that Wrong in politics holds quite a lofty
seat ;
His voice is loudest in the throng when state
conventions meet—
" I nominate !"—he thundering cries; his flunkies
all obey,
In every party gathering his faction wins the day.
This is the riddle to be solved: Who is prepared
to guess,
Why there's so much springs from his brain, so
much from nothingness ?

PESSIMIST.

Disparagement will not explain the power of this
strong man ;
Behind him stand the railroad kings and all the
whiskey clan. .
He rules the bench through caucuses; the ghouls
behind rule him ;
The railroad kings and wiskey rings, they own
him trunk and limb;
The immensity of power he wields is all placed
in his hands
By those huge bloated monied rings no better
than brigands.

But, tell me, is it righteousness in one whose
    trade's the law
To hide his whole religion and his conscience in
    his maw?
I say 'tis not! He has no right, though "Doctor
    of the Laws"
To raise a fratricidal hand against the common
    cause,
A moral cause so sacred! It is treason born of
    Hell
In him or any citizen against it to rebel!
And doubly so if he has lived and fattened and
    grown strong
On the favors of that people, oh it is a cruel
    wrong!
Would he by "technicality" defeat their sovereign
    will,
He should die the death of Judas and then rot on
    some dung hill!
Indeed a patriot unschooled in working for a "fee"
Would gladly give his life, his all, if only he
    could free
Our lovely State from slavery that demon drink
    entails,
Filling with paupers poor-houses; with criminals
    the jails!
And had a spark of gratitude beamed in his sor-
    did breast
He would have said: "Our people speak the
    voice of the Great West,

They who have made me what I am, exalting me
    and mine ;
I'll give my fortune and my life their heart's wish
    to enshrine."
It was a lovely sight to see in that most glorious
    fight
The thousands marching to the front upon the
    side of Right,
Against the powers of Sin and Death ; against the
    hosts of Hell ;
While angels, lauding from the skies, cried :
    " Freemen, ye do well!"

OPTIMIST.

If it be true, the word you speak, then all men
    will agree
Jeff Davis' crime was not more base or mean (his
    treachery)
Than that which we behold to-day of him you
    boldly name,
Who was the people's favorite ; but now (alas!
    the shame !)
Has turned to smite them in the face, used all
    his strength and skill
To strike them down, destroy their power and
    trample on their will!
And he who did this dastard deed will live a with-
    ered man,

A baser act of treachery not since the world began!

PESSIMIST.

The deed is done, the traitor paid and temperance
laws now end;
The party that shall hold control will not again
extend
The privilege (or, rather, right) to speak their
sovereign will
To the "good people of the State;" but it will
cry: "Be still!"
The people will be forced to yield; for "bossism"
will prevail;
Thus every movement for reform will bloom
awhile and fail.

OPTIMIST.

No, no, my friend, though much cast down the
patriots are not dead;
The battle must go on until we crush the serpent's head;
But in this great reverse we see the hand of Providence
Pointing the way to sure success through greater
diligence.

PESSIMIST.

What "diligence" can guard the lamb against the
  wolf's deep wiles ?
To find a pretext for her death he'd trudge a
  thousand miles;
But pretexts are as numerous as stars are in the
  sky,
An·l, as the " Amendment" has gone down, so all
  reforms must die.
The lamb is slain; the surly wolf now gorges on
  his prey;
Black Tyranny usurps a crown and Law is driven
  away !
The law our patriot fathers gave :   "THE PEOPLE
  ARE SUPREME !"
Why if you now e'en name this text the courts
  cry :   " You blaspheme !"
" RED TAPE IS RULER," say the owls; and even
  common sense
Has been clean stricken from the books and rea-
  son's an offense !
A crimsoned shame!   Four starvling tramps have
  power to nullify
The voice of this great Commonwealth—fiat of
  Deity!
Yea, e'en the destinies of all now hang on their
  caprice—

The mask's thrown off; with brazen cheek the
    public voice they scout ;
The unwritten Constitution that our fathers' valor
    won:
THE PEOPLE ARE THE SOVEREIGNS," is swept
    away and gone!
A backward revolution is the devil that we view,
Dethronement of the many and enthronement of
    the few ;
The galling chain of slavery the masses long may
    feel;
No strength may ever break its links of toughest
    tempered steel ;
Where are the mighty people now to trample on
    this deed,
This hellish action of the court, this "bossism"
    gone to seed?
The "Amendment," it is supreme law, who says 'tis
    not rebels!
That traitor to the Commonwealth deserves a
    million hells !
Our rights are trampled in the mire; but (sadder
    cause of grief)
The tribunes of the people to the people's voice
    are deaf!
They veto now our spoken word, usurp the pow-
    er of kings,
And all to serve Unrighteousness (monopolies and
    rings)—

Behold our "grand palladium," our "shield," our
"sure defense,"
Has turned a rattlesnake that strikes with fanged
malevolence!
Strikes the governor, legislature, and the "sovereigns" in the face,
Oh freemen! would that ye could teach the loons
to know their place!

OPTIMIST.

It is a fearful power, I know, that now the ermined
wield:
But the wrong will soon be righted on the moral
battle field.
Believing all is for the best still let us do and dare,
Re-arm us for the holy war and fight against Despair.

PESSIMIST.

You must admit that there are times when freemen should speak out
And not in half a whisper squeak; but boister-
ously shout ;
When their sovereignty is spit upon and courts
transcend their power,
Is't not the time for action then? Is't not the
supreme hour?

9

When the balances are broken and Injustice mounts
    a throne,
Becomes the tyrant of the State, then we should
    not postpone
To raise the cry our fathers did; take their old
    muskets down
And burnish them anew to fight the *Tyrants of the
    Gown.*

Jan. 27, 1883.

THE OUTLOOK.

—o—

THE TRIUMPH OF WOMAN.

OPTIMIST, PESSIMIST.

" Blessed are the meek : for they shall inherit the earth"
—JESUS.

OPTIMIST.

The social evil, half its woes no pen can e'er de-
    pict ;
I honor thee for thy good work Lovina Benedict !
The silent workers, good and true, will bring the
    day about
That we have long been praying for when evil
    shall die out ;
When man shall rise superior to lust and selfish
    greed
And woman shall be disenthralled as nature's God
    decreed ;
She walks the earth an angel now, the light of
    every zone ;
She is the queen of loveliness ; to her is sin un-
    known.

Until by man (her only shield) is confidence betrayed;
In him is all the villainy ; on him the sin be laid !

PESSIMIST.

Right here is where your reasoning, O Opti-
mist's unsound ;
'Tis man to whom she looks for help to lift her
from the ground.
See how Lovina Benedict was pelted with rebuffs
By the Solon Legislators—how a raft of brainless
roughs
(The champions of lager beer, limburger, sauer
kraut,)
Cough, wink and nudge each other and then cold-
ly bow her out!
The whiskey rings must rule, you know, and "personal liberty"
(The only cry that durst be raised) means gross
debauchery;
It means to license dens of shame; open the gates
of Death;
Therefore whoever cries " reform" will only waste
his breath.

OPTIMIST.

Have courage, brother! I behold the dawn of
true reform—
The cause of woman triumphant; God comes not
in the storm.

The quiet workers will prevail with woman in the
van,
And Mary Darwin live to see, and Martha Calla-
nan,
Our daughters honored as our sons; our mothers
(names revered!)
And our good wives—bone of our bone—to us
still more endeared
By the interest that they shall evince in every glo-
rious cause,
Grafting by ballot wisest thought and heart-prayers
on our laws.
And this is all that woman asks: *Make life's arena*
broad—
An ampler field in which to moil, a gleaner for her
God.
Oh why should they wear shackles, those proud
mothers of our sons;
To them far dearer than to us are home and little
ones!
Haste, haste to place within their reach stout
weapons of defense;
That foe of home then quickly dies, demon In-
temperance!
Yea their interests they are greater than man's
selfish interests, far;
Theirs, clearly theirs (flesh, blood and bone) all
human creatures are.
Fond mothers will protect their sons when they
have power to save;

When they can vote, I must believe,   all evil finds
    a grave ;—
Enfranchised woman! with glad songs the event
    will angels hail—
War ends forever; "peace on earth, good will to
    men" prevail.

PESSIMIST.

O friend, how very different all things appear to
    me!
That happy outcome of your dreams this world
    will never see ;
Black Tyranny and Cruelty, while man exists, re-
    main,
And Poverty and Woe and Sin and sordid Lust
    of Gain.
An everlasting conflict fierce rages 'twixt Right
    and Wrong
Despite the voice of prophets old and later poet's
    song ;
Despite all theorizing 'tis the great Creator's plan;
Decay is Nature's finalty and death the doom of
    man ;
And Sin is ever uppermost and Evil triumphs
    still ;
The universal tendency 's not upward, but down
    hill ;
Yea, man has been a tyrant, and fond woman 's
    been misused,

(No one will ever question this) and she 'll be still
    abused;
Though she stands (in her importance in the uni-
    verse) ahead,
The primal source of life on earth (as you have
    justly said);
For, man was given the greater strength by Heav-
    en's supreme decree,
And she must bow submissive lest existence cease
    to be.
This thesis, friend, you will admit: "The stronger
    must prevail."

OPTIMIST.

Will mind succumb to matter then, the cause of
    woman fail?
Superior in the moral realm, the gods must yield
    to her;
Wielding the potent wand of love she will be con-
    queror.
Woman! Call her feeble! there are ripples on
    the deep;
Remove old Ocean from his bed: Why, Hercules,
    you sleep!
She asks no " rights" for selfish ends; for see where
    Love commands
She strikes down "Self"! To shield the weak
    she every ill withstands.
The fear of death has no restraint when Love bids
    her to move;

When Memphis felt the fatal plague behold fond
    woman's love!
She leaps into the jaws of Death, not for the bau-
    ble fame,
Not as the brave " six hundred" charged, her mo-
    tive not the same.
What bore her to the scene of woe?   Her heart
    that never fails!
How many sleep in unknown graves, true Florence
    Nightengales!
Though timid, like the harmless roe when danger
    is afar,
Cool and collected, undismayed, where Death and
    Danger are!
Kate Shelley braves the Storm-fiend's rage, Dark-
    ness, the roaring Flood;
Does Fear deter? Love leads her on ; but who
    protects her?   God!
The social evil must die out when we remove its
    cause ;
See woman then its cause remove when she dic-
    tates the laws !

PESSIMIST.

But, Optimist, the social sin has always cursed
    our earth ;
How little 'tis abated even since the Saviour's
    birth !
Or since poor Mary Magdalene beheld its antidote

In him, the true Redeemer ! And what now (though
  woman vote)
Can be done to lift the fallen from the slums and
  hold them up ?
Oh I'd rejoice to see removed the poisoned, bitter cup
That the millions (darling daughters fondest parents doted on)
Now drink, are lost, " abandoned !" Oh that day
  for them might dawn !
Egyptian night enshrouds them.   Like the giddy
  butterfly,
In a blaze of sensuality, behold them flit and die !

OPTIMIST.

The answer, Pessimist, is given when you the
  Saviour name ;
The antidote is love ! 'Twill all the Magdalenes
  reclaim ;
The love engrafted on our laws that beams from
  woman's soul,
The love that Christ imparted, 'twill the universe
  control !
Will lift the abandoned from the slums.   The
  Heaven-sent antidote
Will be applied to every ill when woman casts her
  vote.
For drunkards grand asylums, and for the aban-
  doned homes ;

When she prevails we hear the shout :   " Behold
    the Master comes ;"
Yea,this (His second coming) mighty prophets old
    foresaw
When He shall reign a thousand years and love
    shall be the law!
Not anything that she deems wrong will she (law-
    maker) do;
And righteousness placed in the laws will curb the
    greedy few—
Will give the toiling many all the products of
    their toil; '
Will break the foul monopolies : land, railroad,
    standard oil—
Remove the cause of social vice ; give all a work ;
    and give
To all the certain prospect that by labor they shall
    live.

PESSIMIST.

You are too sanguine in your hopes, kind Opti-
    mist, by far;
For woman is as greedy as all other creatures are ;
And she will wink at evil if that evil bring her
    wealth ;
And she will be as ready quite to overreach by
    stealth ;
Corruption, too, in politics, will not be less ram-
    pant ;

Old England has a queen you know, with heart
    of adamant;
Beholds the woes of Ireland ; beholds the millions
    die
Of hunger, robbed, oppressed ; and yet her gra-
    cious eyes are dry !

OPTIMIST.

Man is the first when evil comes to grasp the sin-
    ful cup;
When evil dies, say, who is then the last to give
    it up ?
The wave that drowns King Alcohol drowns the
    tobacco fiend ;
Who last, I ask, is't he or she that from its pow-
    er is weaned?
And though you blame the British queen the
    fault rests not with her ;
For England's sins arraign her lords and her Prime
    Minister.
Let suffrage be extended in Great Britain ; let all
    men
(And women too) go to the polls as equals, and
    right then
A mighty revolution would the world at once be-
    hold,
And Ireland would rejoice indeed with blessings
    manifold.

When this shall come about, dear friend, in every
  Christian land
God's kingdom we behold in fact; the armies all
  disband:
The world we see united in a sisterhood of states;
A congress of all nations meet (peaceful confed-
  erates!)
To settle all disputed points. The sword will nev-
  ermore
Be drawn from out its scabbard to be stained with
  human gore!

PESSIMIST.

When Selfishness has ceased to be, and kings
  are overthrown,
And when the toiling millions stand together and
  are one,
We may hope to see the happy time that you anticipate
When each shall seek the other's good and all co-
  operate
To lift the helpless from the dust and care for the
  distressed;
To give the enfeebled pleasant homes and to the
  toilers rest.

OPTIMIST.

That blessed day is sure to come and now is almost here

When Might shall cease to be the law and none
   will domineer;
When Righteousness will reign on earth and
   "right" the only end,
And man will be no longer "lord"; but woman's
   trusted friend ;—
And it is plain and plausible that cruel, bestial
   Force
Has in this age of Intellect now nearly run his
   course ;
The weaker are the stronger, and the mighty are
   the weak—
The world is newly peopled ; its inhabitants the
   meek.

Feb. 25, 1883.

ENGLAND AND EGYPT.

——o——

LAWYER JONES, FARMER SMITH.

" *And they shall beat their swords into plowshares and
their spears into pruning-hooks: nation shall not
lift up sword against nation, neither shall they learn
war any more.*" —ISAIAH.

LAWYER JONES.

Right stormy news to-day, friend Smith,
　We have from Alexandria;
The English fleet has opened fire
　Effectively and grandly!

The British, ever wide awake,
　Have made a demonstration
That must add glory to their name
　And shekels to the nation.

FARMER SMITH.

Jones, since I had my only son
　Slain with a shell at Shiloh
I feel how terrible are wars—
　They've lost to me their halo.

What have the men of Egypt done
　To stir up such a clangor?

It must be some great crime, of course,
  To rouse thus England's anger?

The crime, as I have heard, is this:
  The Fellah are declaring
They cannot pay the Khedive's debts
  To Rothschild and to Baring.

Eight dollars to the acre now
  Is the enormous levy
Of tax they pay upon their lands—
  They claim it is too heavy.

The Fellah, like the Irish, dare
  To kick against their masters—
This is the crime that brought them war
  With all its dire disasters.

The farmers, let them stick to work—
  The war is incidental,
A mere attempt on England's part
  To help enforce the rental.

For " honest payment" she declares
  Of bonded obligation ;
And now she points her Gatling guns
  Against Repudiation.

FARMER SMITH.

This howl for "honesty" by wolves
    Is thinly-disguised knavery—
The most dishonest things on earth
    Are war and human slavery.

The maxim of all men should be
    (Now hear me plainly state it):—
Whatever fetters Liberty
    We should repudiate it !

No bond or mortgage can wipe out
    The " higher obligation"
(" Life, Liberty, and Happiness")
    Writ in our Declaration.

" All tax" (says English law itself—
    No better law had Sparta)
" Is but a voluntary gift"—
    Vide old *Magna Charta !*

Let Albion proclaim in tones
    That all mankind may hear her,
And Ireland, India, Africa,
    And Egypt loudly cheer her:—

" Only a voluntary gift
    (The tax or rent) you may give—
Old England guarantees your right
    And holds in check the Khedive.

" He shall not raise a hand to place
  A yoke upon the many—
They shall not be constrained to give
  To Idleness a penny.".

But now the shameful fact appears
  That England stands to fetter
The multitude—the Shylock's " bond"
  Enforces to the letter.

Is Shylock sweltering in the ranks
  Fighting old England's battles?
Oh, no! He snugly *stays at home.*
  Who fight? Why, "human chattels !"

False Albion's boast of many years :
  " No slave can breathe in Britain"—
But Ireland is a land of slaves
  To England's shame be it written.

More abject is their slavery
  Than that of Negro chattels ;
Yet Irish blood and bravery
  Win England's "glorious battles."

This is the shoe that pinches most :
  That toilers should belabor
Their toiling brothers and forget
  Their duty to their neighbor.

The " Royal Irish Regiment"
  To Egypt now is sailing,

10

To forge for her the self-same chains
    That Ireland is bewailing.

Throw down your guns, Green Erin's sons!
    Stand by your toiling brothers!
Think of the suffering ones at home—
    Your sisters and your mothers!

LAWYER JONES.

Why, Smith, you rave like one insane;
    The English Constitution
Should be the model for our own.
    Give us a revolution

That brings a "stronger Government,"
    One that will be emphatic,
To hold the workingmen in check—
    We grow too democratic.

" *Vox populi, vox Dei!*" yell
    The ragged, hungry rabble—
It is more int'resting to hear
    A thousand ganders gabble!

The British Government is right
    In putting Egypt under;
And "No Rent" Ireland, too, will quail
    Before the English thunder;

For Egypt and old Ireland both
    Deserve the healing plaster

Of shot, and shell, and minie balls—
Toilers must have a master!

FARMER SMITH.

Friend Jones, your frankness is sublime;
You bravely tell your story—
Our fathers, if they'd heard you talk,
Had shot you for a Tory!

This Tory smell is in the air ;
Aristocratic stinkers
(The race of rotten millionaires)
Now play the role of " thinkers."

They squeak through every venal press,
And howl against the "strikers,"
And rave about the " dangerous class,"
Still hounding on their *he curs!*

And many honest men like you
Re-echo their palaver,
You love Brittania so well ?
I'm willing you shall have her.

My grandsire fought at Bunker Hill;
I hate (Darwin explain it!)
The name of " Lords and Monarchy ;"
Like Milton, I disdain it !

O Pym, Vane, Hampden, Eliot
Call, with your ancient summons,

The traitor Straffords of to-day
    Before a patriot Commons!

The work those glorious martyr's did,
    True Englishmen, Oh heed it!
A bold handwriting's on the wall—
    Aristocrats may read it.

That writing is to this effect:
    "THE DAYS OF LORDS ARE NUMBERED!"
We plant just privilege for all
    Upon the ground they've cumbered—

The land is for the men that plow,
    The water for the seamen;
One class alone upon the earth—
    That class we hail them " FREEMEN."

All " peoples" shall be joined as one—
    United as one nation;
Democracy shall rule the world,
    A great Confederation.

The guaranty shall be :—No soul
    Shall ever be molested—
All obligations rest upon
    Friendships disinterested.

All "legal debts" shall be unknown;
    Known only " debts of honor ;"
No " interest notes," no mortgages;
    The State no "bonds" upon her.

The rule, then, of the " Prince of Peace"
    Must end all litigation—
All grave misunderstandings cease
    In friendly arbitration.

Old England soon will take the lead
    In this grand revolution;
Her workingmen are now agreed
    To end all destitution.

Her lands will be divided up
    In farms of twenty acres;
The glorious English-speaking race
    Will be the world's law-makers.

The shell is now about to break
    (This hope, O toilers, cherish!),
The New will rise a bright Phœnix,
    The Old will shortly perish!

LAWYER JONES.

Well, Farmer Smith, you've made a speech
    (I tell it to your credit),
More eloquent it could not be
    If e'en a lawyer had said it.

I'm now convinced it would be well
    (While England watches strangers),
It would be well tor Uncle Sam
    To keep an eye on Grangers.

July 13, 1882.

CRIME'S CARNIVAL.

——o——

LAWYER JONES, FARMER SMITH.

" It is a frequent sight to see
High dangling from a limb
A ghastly wretch—this thing to me
Is joy—though grief to him."
Popular Song of the Period.

LAWYER JONES.

Last night we did a noble job:
Des Moines, transformed into a mob,
Strung up another murderous fiend—
Although the Sheriff intervened
To save the wretch from righteous wrath,
We followed hot upon his path
And sent him to his just reward:
We left him dangling to a cord!

FARMER SMITH.

Honor to Sheriff Littleton!
The love of all true men he won—
The grand old soldier! schooled to do
His duty! to his country true!
No truckling, base time-server can
Appreciate so brave a man!

LAWYER JONES.

What did he then?   I'll tell you, sir:
He stept betwixt the murderer
And justice that we were about,
In wholesome sort, to measure out!
Though my profession is the law,
And from it I subsistence draw,
I see the crying need to-day
Of putting lawlessness away—
And not by costly, bungling courts
Where barefaced Bribery resorts,
Until it has become a shame,
A judge or jury, e'en to name;
But by the people in their might
Dethroning Wrong enthroning Right—
And I can see no better course
Than to revive the *Law of Force*.

FARMER SMITH.

Jones, now you strike an ugly job;
Mob will be met by counter mob.
You overthrow society;
You bring in War and Anarchy;
You sink our country down as low
As barbarous, mob-cursed Mexico!

LAWYER JONES.

There is a power behind the throne;
'Tis time the power were felt and known!

See lawlessness triumphant here
In city, country, everywhere!
See our kind parson's " gentlemen"
Have closed, as yet, *hardly one den,*
And drunkenness runs riot still
In spite of law and people's will!
If Elder Lucas would but know,
There is a way to overthrow
The lawless fiends whom even Hell
Would scarcely give a place to dwell.
They care for country, right and laws
No more than does a crow that caws—
With traitorous audacity
They stab the people's sovereignty;
They thus haul down the flag—why not
Just "shoot" the villains "on the spot?"
Their rotten carcasses should swing,
And dangle to a hempen string!
The people, in their glorious might,
En masse, should organize some night,
Tear down, demolish, overturn,
Wipe out, obliterate and burn
Each den where Lawlessness is shown
To reign defiant on the throne.

FARMER SMITH.

Jones, I (like you) regret to see
So much of vice and misery:
The star-route steal, and then the farce

(The Dorsey trial) ten times worse!
Yet we can but approximate,
Not wholly reach a perfect State— ;
Against the tidal-wave of wrong
There is a counter-current strong—
The storm of sin is at its worst:
We see the cloud above us burst—
Signs are propitious in the air ;
Now soon the weather will be fair.

LAWYER JONES.

What are those signs?   I'm surely blind—
Hugely benighted in my mind!
Still you may (or Professor Tice),
Ward off the dread cyclone of vice,
That strikes against Des Moines as fell
As did the storm-fiend smite Grinnell.

FARMER SMITH.

The signs are these: hatred of crime
That now is horribly sublime—
There is abroad a sense of right,
That gives the patriot true delight—
Behold the prohibition wave
Insures the vile beer-fiend a grave!
Impatience, you yourself display
That lawlessness be done away—
The people's will—this is the word—

The voice of Might—sword of the Lord—
The wand of Peace!—The common throng,
That love the right and hate the wrong,
They soon will raise their hands on high,
Swear for their homes to live and die ;—
Our country! It shall rise and beam
Far brighter than our Fathers' dream ;
No need of mobs and brutish Force!
Ah, Jones, the remedy is worse
Than the disease. A better plan
The Son of God and Son of Man
Has given to us : "*Do good for ill!*"
To sin's wild waves cry, "Peace; be still!"
Not maudlin sentiment He spoke ;
But bread of highest truth He broke.
Philosophy—the grandest kind—
Beamed from His God-illumined mind;
And mankind soon will wake to see
The depth of His philanthropy.

LAWYER JONES.

Friend Smith, your talk is vague and wild ;
Be something definite compiled !
Your " healing remedy," forsooth,
Should strongly smack of pungent truth ;
Facts, you well know, are stubborn things
For common men and crowned kings ;
We facts of vice and murder meet
Now every day upon the street ;—

The cause is plain ; but what's the cure ?
Not sentimental pills, I'm sure;
Ropes and revolvers, fire and sword
Will bring us nearer to the Lord !

FARMER SMITH.

The cause, friend Jones, is not so plain ;—
How may we social health regain ?
Remove, of vice and crime, the cause,
Then we shall have no need of laws.

LAWYER JONES.

Do I admit it ? Yes, I do!
What you've just said is grandly true !

FARMER SMITH.

O friend, we should not sleep, till we
Have felled the poison Upas tree !
The way to help strike down the cause
Of sin, is to uphold the laws ;—
Our noble Sheriff hit the plan :
" *Stand by the laws!*"—God bless the man!
And when we find onr laws are lame
Then let us better statutes frame !

LAWYER JONES.

But Smith, the laws we can't enforce ;

You see, Des Moines grows worse and
    worse—
See sixty-five saloonists stand
Defiant of our loud command!
We can't suppress a tippling hell ;
Because the " gentlemen" rebel.
These sixt-five out-flank, you see,
Twelve hundred—our majority!
Behold, Tom. Jefferson a fool !
Majorities have ceased to rule ;
Here sixty-five law-breakers gloat,
Swagger and swear—seize by the throat
The City Fathers—drive the Mayor,
As do the butchers drive a steer !
They on the altar pile greenbacks
And lo! "His Honor" melts like wax!
The people rule? 'Tis not the case ;
Old Mammon governs in their place!

FARMER SMITH.

Ah, public sentiment is strong—
All powerful to throttle wrong ;
This is enough—raise no rude hand—
See Mayors cower before her wand—
See City Fathers quake with fear—
See Legislators hark and hear—
See Congressmen obey her nod ;
(Her voice, Jones, is the voice of God!)
And Presidents and Kings succumb
If she but sternly snap her thumb !

LAWYER JONES.

Well Farmer Smith forgive my heat;
I see my words were indiscreet;—
The farmer (Hercules) at last
(This globe upon his shoulders vast)
Moves forward bearing all along—
Smith, you were right and I was wrong!
Your words of wisdom I commend;
The law, the law's our truest friend—
In what I spoke there's this great flaw—
That lawless mobs can uphold law—
It is not true! May mob rule cease;
The people's will enforce, O, Peace!

Sept. 23, 1882.

THE "NEW PARTY."

———o———

LAWYER JONES, FARMER SMITH.

" *Unite or die.*"— OLD CONTINENTAL MOTTO.

LAWYER JONES.

Ah, Farmer Smith, I've heard sad news,
Enough to give us all the blues:
The court, obedient to the lash
Of party leaders and to " cash"
Have knocked the " Amendment" into pi—
The parties—they deserve to die !

FARMER SMITH.

The parties !   Let us say, friend Jones,
'Tis not the parties ; but the drones
(Knaves that on public plunder thrive
And fatten in the party hive)
That ever do the " dirty work"—
They flourish the assassin's dirk
And stab the Amendment ; not the swarm
That keep the party bee-hives warm.
The parties are quite good enough—
Are made of very best of stuff.
All parties, Jones, embrace good men ;

But swine fed in the party pen
(Corruption gaunt, with ravenous Greed,
Begot this home-destroying breed)
Deserve the metaphoric knife—
Take theirs and not the parties' life!

LAWYER JONES.

Health nursed the party babes ; Decay
Embraces them (old hags!) to-day:
They merit death ten million times
For thrice ten million horrid crimes!

FARMER SMITH.

To o'erthrow parties, build anew,
Is just the hardest thing to-do—
Nor you, nor I can pull them down ;
They perish when the millions frown—
Disband when they have ceased to bear
The people's standard high in air.

LAWYER JONES.

The people's standard! Why, my friend
The people's rule is at an end
Unless they, wrathful, rise and slay
The rotten parties right away!

FARMER SMITH.

If " rotten" they'll disintegrate
And fall apart of their own weight ;—
They droop and die if they engage
To stop the progress of the age ;
Thus fell the Whigs when Webster spoke
At Marshfield: " Bind the hateful yoke
Upon the blacks, O Whigs ! Commend
The South and stand the Oppressor's friend!
Then Whiggery felt the cruel knife—
And from that wound escaped its life !

LAWYER JONES.

Ah 'twas a fearful gash, friend Smith !

FARMER SMITH.

The slave-lord's interest was the pith
And marrow of the great man's speech ;—
And, Jones, class interest is the leech
That saps the life of patriot zeal—
(Attachment to the Commonweal)
And though it nerves a sordid few,
To move the masses 'Twill not do.

LAWYER JONES.

Did not the party (that may own
As father, patriot Jefferson,)

Attach itself to Slavery's car
And thus bring on the civil war!

FARMER SMITH.

For seventy years the "public weal"
Was hailed the popular appeal—
Great Jackson raised his patriot hand;
" The Union shall eternal stand!
Avaunt! treason-inflated ghouls!
I'll hang ye, nullifying fools!"
But Jackson died; " bosses" arose,
The slave-lords' friends, their country's
    foes—
'Twas then we heard the welkin ring
The horrid yell: " Cotton is King!"
And cotton planters held the reins,
Were "all in all" except the brains:—
What fools! to think that their command
Could be the law of this great land !
What fools! to think one interest small
Could hold this mighty world in thrall!

LAWYER JONES.

Friend Smith, it is the same to-day;
The whiskey mongers curbed of sway,
The mercenary dogs, rebel;
They raise the hateful " rebel yell "—

And see owl Democrats proclaim
" Free Whiskey " in the people's name—
And owl Republicans the same!
Both Whigs and Democrats of old
Sought shelter in the slave-lord's fold—
(But Douglas—patriot soul and true—
From partnership with Wrong withdrew)
Just as to-day all parties beg
A seat upon a lager-keg!
And history thus repeats itself;—
The parties! pile them on the shelf!
Sell out, sell out "boss" Democrats!
O herd of noisy, ravenous rats!
Yield all things to the beer-fiend's will—
Ye masses, bow obedient still !

FARMER SMITH.

See, Progress halts not—looks not back ;
The party whips now vainly crack!
Home slays Saloon ; though ermined cranks
Succumb to threats of vile beer-tanks—
The Court a siege-gun; brewers load it;
They fire it off; alas! explode it !
" Boss " Wright stood by to prime the gun—
His corpse lies stinking in the sun!

LAWYER JONES.

Smith, what of last November's vote?
The whiskey-mongers o'er it gloat—

It spoke in thunder tones :   " Farewell
To temperance laws and welcome Hell. "

FARMER SMITH.

Not while Columbia has a soul
Will whiskey-mongers have control!
Not while a Christian impulse thrills
To nerve our patriotic wills !
The car of Progress goes not back ;
But ever forward on the track—
Yes, onward, forward, though up hill,
But onward, upward, forward still!
And Reformation comes to earth
When man is ripe to hail its birth—
But, when it comes, it comes to stay
And "bossism" cannot drive 't away.

LAWYER JONES.

Your logic's soundness, Smith, I doubt;—
Who was it counted Tilden out?
A Reformation was that not—
A Reformation Hell-begot!
Corruption of the blackest kind,
And usurpation deep-designed !
By which the people were befooled;
Chicane and bare-faced Bribery ruled—
And office-holding harpies dared
To trample on the Flag : declared
The nation's vote a nullity;
And now the after-birth we see—

A tyrant Court's hateful decree!

FARMER SMITH.

'Twas Tilden!   He's the dolt to blame!
His coward action, what a shame!
Had he e'en breathed one manly breath ;
Cried " my just rights or martyr death,
Stood bravely for the common cause—
The Constitution and the Laws—
Had whispered but the faintest word
Jacksonian—'twould have been heard!

LAWYER JONES.

But still the Muse of History
Will write it down :   " Black Infamy ! "
Ah, 'tis a blot, a deep disgrace
That time nor distance can efface—
A trick of "bossism " and chicane
Most criminal and most insane !

FARMER SMITH.

But you admit all that I claim :
The " rank and file" are not to blame
For what the leaders madly do;
The " parties," then, are *good* and *true !*
I say the parties, each to each,
Are as alike as peach to peach ;
Hosts, hosts of sheep house in each fold;

Slay, slay the wolves we there behold !
The " bosses" (Weaver and Judge Wright)
Are as alike as white's like white ;—
While man is man 'twill be as now ;
The only question asked is: " How
May I attain the ends I seek ?"—
(The words of party knave and sneak)'
Show him the path to place and power ;
He'll walk that path before an hour !
His "views " are very quick to change—
See how the Courts knelt to the Grange !

LAWYER   JONES.

But now Corruption holds the reins ;
A cranky Court, devoid of brains,
Spits squarely in the people's face—
And we must bow to this disgrace !
What was Jeff Davis' crime to this ?
What e'en the traitor Judas' kiss ?
Why they were virtues when compared
To what a brainless Court have dared.
Smith, 'tis a miracle amends
Those knaves—makes them the people's
      friends !

FARMER   SMITH.

The secret of success, Jones, lies
Just in this one word :   " Organize."—
The Eagle hears Reynard's command

When Reynard wields a fire brand—
"Grand Army"—it is listened to—
E'en Congress hears the *boys in blue.*
To Courts, the Grangers' speech was terse—
"The Dartmouth College case reverse!"
The Courts obeyed.   Monopoly
Then bowed its head and bent its knee.
Whose fault is't now if farmers groan?
Nobody's fault except their own!
The whiskey interest is combined;
Monopolies have but one mind—
All monied "rings" consolidate
And march *en masse* against the State;
The Courts are cringing slaves to these;
But we may free them if we please;
Our willing tribunes they become
If we but strenly crook a thumb—
Then Jones whose fault is't if the host
Of temperance has the victory lost?

LAWYER JONES.

Clearly not ours!   We spoke aloud;
The vote!—Oh I am grandly proud
Of its proportions!   We may found
A splendid party on that ground!
The temperance banner now unfurled
Will wave triumphant o'er the world.

FARMER SMITH.

Our Fathers' voice long time was heard

Shout " Loyalty to George the Third !"
They organized for legal ends ;
The bough may break ; but first it bends,
The loyal " Sons of Liberty "
Became sworn foes to Royalty—
Old party ties are hard to break ;
A last resort when men forsake
Old party comrads—friends of years
Companions of their hopes and fears—
Parties break up like ice in spring ;
Then " loyal subjects " fight their king.
But, Jones, the maxim best to know
When we'd build parties, is, " go slow; "
Had Greenbackers pursued this course,
The greenback wave had rolled with force;
It might have risen to overflow
And drown Production's hated foe,
Monopoly.   Its force was lost
In gathering up a " Weaver Host."

LAWYER JONES.

Say, do I understand you now ?
First organize ; and (you avow,)
A Warren's or Henry's voice may bring
Us up in arms against the King ?

FARMER SMITH.

A rivulet at first we see,
The Mississippi finally ;

First count the cost, then build the house—
The mountain's progeny's a mouse ;
Loud groans accompanied its pains ;
God speaks, but not where Tumult reigns!

LAWYER JONES.

Your views, friend Smith, are nobly grand;—
Here, Granger, here's my warm right hand !

Feb. 10, 1883.

THE TRUCE.

——o——

•LAWYER JONES, FARMER SMITH.

" Cheap money will solve the problem of free trade.—"
WENDELL PHILLIPS.

LAWYER JONES,

Glad tidings, Smith! Our statesmen say
There soon will rise a happier day
When farmers shall receive their due,—
How goes the battle, friend, with you?
Has not our Kasson made it plain
That with protection we regain
A healthful life to Industry
And farmers better times shall see?
Our Allison has fairly shown
That Greenbacks must be overthrown
And bankers must be given the sway
To bring in the millennial day.
The bankers' promisory notes
Will pay for wheat and corn and oats,
And move the tons of beef and pork,
Affording farmers ample work ;
And when our bonded debt is paid
Secure will bankers' notes be made

By railroad bonds and watered stocks
And mortgages on city blocks,
And " iron-clads " on farms and homes
(The fruitful source whence interest comes)
And thus backed up those notes will stand
The " money of our favored land; "
And Uncle Sam ('tis understood)
Will still delight to make them good;
" Receivable for Federal tax "
Still gladly stamp upon their backs;
But "lawful money ". (Greenback notes
That paid our glorious *blue coats*)
He will put down!   No mere fiat;
Let government endorse " wild cat. "

FARMER SMITH.

A farmer, you, and tell the truth !
A " cranky " idiot, forsooth,
A lunatic not fit to live,
Would still know better than to give
Kasson's and Allison's quack pills
To purge our country of her ills.
To " help the people " they pretend;
To serve the millionaries, the end !

LAWYER JONES.

Smith, how you rave ; Those men
        doubt
True patriots) would bring about

Most prosperous times.   Statesmen indeed;
They know just what the people need.
The Greenback (Oh, most dangerous thing!)
Builds up a governmental ring.   ·

FARMER SMITH.

A monstrous "ring" your fears present ;
The " people are the government"—
Ring may they be !   Upon my word
You give to toil a two-edged sword
When promissory notes you hold
To be a money good as gold.
Our government deign to receive
Bank-notes for taxes!   Jones, believe,
This precedent will rise and slay
Old King Monopoly some day.

LAWYER JONES.

Your words amaze me!   Let me hear
You, farmer Smith, make this appear.

FARMER SMITH.

Let farmers' notes (backed by good lands
Like bankers' notes are backed by bonds)
Be put afloat : the government
Give them endorsement that is lent
To Bankers' notes!   " Not to refuse
The farmers' notes for excise dues. ''

A tax of one per cent be paid .
(The same that on bank-notes is laid)
Then bankers' ten per cent is gone
And Usury has lost the throne !

LAWYER JONES.

'Tis so,, indeed, I must confess !
Our Allison will favor this !
He surely will; a Western man
Cannot oppose so just a plan ;
Our lands are good security :
The notes of farmers then will be
As good as national bank scrip.
With such " sound currency " the ship
Of state will ever ride secure ;
Our liberties, for aye, endure.

FARMER SMITH.

Well, Jones, I am surprised to see
You grasp this truth so heartily—
My prejudice had grown so strong
'Gainst lawyers, that I thought them wrong
In everything.   But now I own
Rank prejudice is overthrown.
Yet, Jones, believe, in this fair land,
May Free-trade and Protection stand
Right side by side and hand in hand.

LAWYER JONES,

Oh, pshaw ! You raise too big a " boo !"
This paradox cannot be true—
Free-trade ! Protection !—are not these,
Friend Smith, direct antipodes ?

FARMER SMTIH.

Not so ; cheap money will untie
The knot of your perplexity.

LAWYER JONES.

Why, Smith, how is it ?—let me hear ;
I doubt if you can make this clear.

FARMER SMITH.

Let " operatives " associate
And form a " body-corporate "
And put afloat their legal " notes."
The care the government devotes
To bankers' scrip let it concede
To these, and lo ! they're cash indeed !
This " workmen's scrip " will build up, then,
Big factories for working men ;
These factories so built will be
The government's " security ;"
But not in factory, not in farm
The safety ; but the toiler's arm ;

Securest pledge to common weal
Are Labor's plighted hand and seal!
Yet all the government need care
Is to receive its annual share
Of profits—just the *one per cent,*
Of interest due the government :
'Tis all the bankers give to-day ;
'Tis all the factory hands should pay.
We reach our highest " duty " when
We most protect our working-men ;
Cheap money and protection meet—
Great Britain cannot then compete
With Labor here.   When Labor owns
The factories, she grinds the bones
Of Britain's money-lords and brings
Down from their thrones the factory kings;
Free be our ports!   We now defy
King Gold and King Monopoly !

LAWYER JONES.

I see the point; our working-men
Receiving all the profits then,
Our goods forever undersell
All foreign goods.   We thus expel
All foreign wares.   Our toilers stand
The monarchs of our happy land !

June 4, 1882.

BROTHERHOOD.

———o———

LAWYER JONES AND FARMER SMITH.

*"If ye salute your brethren only what do ye more than
others ? Do not even the publicans so ?"*—JESUS

LAWYER JONES.

Well, Farmer Smith, our nation's birth
We hail to-day,—the Glorious Fourth!
All men with one united voice,
Throw up their beavers and rejoice—
Odd Fellows and Free Masons march :
The Plumed Knights, the Royal Arch,
United are each brotherhood
In one grand purpose to do good.

FARMER SMITH.

"Unchristian " is the fittest term
To designate each narrow firm,
United for a selfish end
Is just their highest recommend—
True patriots, Jones, 'tis understood,
Associate for the general good.

LAWYER JONES.

And, Farmer Smith, great good we see
The fruit of each fraternity :
Poor widows in their gratitude,
And orphans bless each brotherhood.

FARMER SMITH.

You would as well reside in Hell
As in a lodge-cursed town to dwell—
Not a friend you ever meet ;
Not a neighbor on the street—
But an alien you will be
Unknown in that community—
Ask a favor, you are spurned ;
Or like Servetus, you are burned—
Or " hanged and quartered " if you dare
To crave a breath of vital air !

LAWYER JONES.

Why Farmer Smith, 'tis indiscreet
For you to talk so on the street ;
The lodge---the family made large---
"To help each other," is the charge.

FARMER SMITH.

Those selfish orders in their greed,
Are Judaism gone to seed---

Their deeps of mystery conceal
The brainless, eyeless lamper-eel
That fattens on the life and health
Of the depleted Commonwealth.
Away with tribes! Give me a State
In which all interests congregate !
Hence, monkish recluse, to thy cave !
Hence, selfish "brother," to thy grave !
Hail Patriot ! Thy life and health
(Loving thy neighbor as thyself)
Are wedded to the Commonwealth :
'As comprehensive thy regard
As is the love of Christ our Lord.
How narrow these ! Each clannish "Knight"
Is sworn to trample on the right—
Is sworn with all his strength to cling
To sordid interests of a "ring"---
All true philanthropy must fail
While still the cry is "Saxon," "Gael !"

LAWYER JONES.

These orders were not built to fence
Out Love and true Benevolence.

FARMER SMITH.

Ah, neighbor Jones, dark shadow they
(The substance long since passed away)

Dark shadow of a cruel horde
That scourged the nations with the sword,
Out-growth of savagery, turmoil,
Banditti ravaging for spoil,
And sworn (with noose on neck) to stand
True to the "brothers" of their band.
Few, only few, the clans protect;
The many suffer their neglect---
Build up a Christian Brotherhood
That will the human race include---
Let not an orphan child be found
Uncared for on the top of ground;
Let not a widow e'er be sent
To poor-house from her tenement---
Provide for them abundantly,
And not in name of "Charity."
Vile "Charity"---a word accurst---
Of odious words the very worst!

LAWYER JONES.

It will be done! I have no doubt
The lodge will help bring this about---
She educates men to dispense
Their gifts with true munificence;
She educates them to bestow
Their wealth to lighten human woe;
Teacher of love and righteousness,
She lifts the helpless from distress.

FARMER SMITH.

Not so; the contrary is true :
While lodges still exist, will you
Behold the members of those bands
Ever attempt to tie the hands
Of "overseers of the poor,"
Begrudging e'en the scanty store
The law provides, cursing the tax
As "onerous burden" on their backs,
The lodge (a state within a State,
A "one-horse" body corporate)
Wheels them along.   They soundly sleep
While orphans starve and widows weep ;
But could the lodge be done away
Then every citizen' would pray
For full provision for the poor,
For widows, orphans, ample store ;
Would hail a true fraternity
Of every soul on land and sea ; ·
I trust that this may shortly be.

LAWYER JONES.

Perfect the State !   It is decreed
That clanship dies when dies its need.

FARMER SMITH.

What conquerer, neighbor Jones, will reign
Above those "rings" a Charlemagne?

Who, out of narrowness, bring forth
A New Jerusalem on earth?

LAWYER JONES.

The "Gentile" millions when awake,
Those narrow "Judean rings" will break ;—
But I perceive that we agree ;
So let us join the jubilee.

July 10th 17 2.

ALBION'S DISGRACE

----o----

The bodies of Egyptian soldiers were hacked and
slashed almost out of resemblance to humanity by
the long broadswords of the English Life Guards.
One young] Egyptian officer still held]an unlighted
cigarette in his stiffened fingers.- -*Associated Press
Dispatch, Aug. 31st, 1882.*

Morals are the basis of politics. Perhaps my step
will divide my party ; but I cannot abandon my
principles from any regard for my party or my affection for my friends.--*John Bright.*

Say, was it worse to slay with dynamite
The Russian Czar, or stab with cruel knife
Lord Cavendish and Burke, than thus to hack
And slash and hew with murderous great swords
Beyond resemblance to humanity
The inoffensive agriculturists,
That crouch in rooflesss huts along the Nile ?
Was not the life of that young officer,
That fell beneath the merciless broadsword,
Still holding an unlighted cigarette,
Clutched in his stiffened fingers, worth as much
As that of Queen Victoria or her son
Whom she restrained from hastening to the front ?
Then why did she not hold the nation back

From this most foul and barberous enterprise?
Is royal blood too sacred to be spilt?
Ah, human blood's too sacred to be spilt!
The queen bethought herself to curb her son;
To"negative his rage for human gore!
Indeed! was this the cause of the decree
Against her scion's arming for the fight?
It should have been the cause and motive grand
A motive worthy of the "Christian Queen"
That she is styled by those who worship her.
She should have said:

        " Edward, my royal son,
Die, if need be, as Jesus died for men;
Live (while thou livest) a good Samaritan;
Bind up the wounds of those fallen by the way;
And nurse thou e'en the afflicted with Black
      Death,
Though thy own life be forfeit to the act,
Yet never wrong of life thy fellow man;
Give up thine own to bless humanity,
But look with horror on aggressive war;
For war is horrible in any guise—
The greatest evil that afflicts mankind—
'Tis always wrong, and never, never right!
Bring joy, my son, to all the suffering poor;
Forgive the debtor, as thou'dst be forgiven;
Abolish rent as an immoral tax,
And usury as robbery most foul;
Take in thy arms the helpless everywhere—

Like Howard, find the darkest prison hells,
Open their grates and let God's sunlight in;
Lift up the lowly and make glad all hearts ;
Cry : 'Wars, be thou no more !' 'And O, grim
    swords,
Change thou to plowshares ! spears to pruning
    hooks!
And Peace, and Love and Brotherhood prevail!"

The world united as one family,
Speaking, by telegraph and telephone,
Congratulations to enfranchised States,
Saying, "O, India, stand upon thy feet !
O, Africa, behold thou art a queen !
Thy Egypt is the freest of the free,
After dire bondage of three thousand years,
To Medes and Persians, Greeks, Romans and
    Turks!
Green Ireland, hail! Thy ancient liberties
Are guaranteed by England's gracious voice;
Behold! again angelic hosts rejoice,
Loud chanting, 'Peace on Earth, Good Will to
    Men !'
The constellations clap their hands and sing;
The sons of God shout peans of great joy !"

'T is thus he would have said—the aged chief
Of whom, great Albion, thou art rightly proud !
John Bright ! one glorious act has given to thee
A seat above all sceptered royalty ;
Thy grand refusal to record thy name

In favor of the cruel, causeless war
'Gainst Egypt! Thou, great Commoner hast
    stood
Ever for Peace and Human Brotherhood.

The hungry vultures of the Christian North
Swoop down on Islam with unchristian swords—
St. George's cross, emblem of savagery,
Displayed from mastheads high o'er the canal,
Highway to India, through which huge ships
Pass and repass, freighted with stolen goods
And guns and bombs, artillery to hold
The tributary nations still enchained
Behind the chariot of Nobility,
To grace the triumph of the "privileged few"
That flaunt their wealth and trample upon Toil.
The commons reap no good, no benefit
From England's wars and savage tyranny.
What wages do her soldiers get who fight
And maim and murder for a livelihood?
Who slash and hack with merciless broadswords
Out of all semblance to humanity
The youthful patriots of feeble states.
What wages do her seamen get, who moil
On deck and in the rigging, through the heat
Of tropic suns, or where old Boreas' sleet
Cuts their rough faces, or the hurricane
Sweeps by and leaves them clinging to the
    wreck?
Her "Life Guards" force poor farmers to pay
    "rents;"

Who grasp the rents as soon as they are paid ?
The " Lord his God"—British Nobility !
Life guards, forsooth !   Vile murderers the name
That fitly designates her hounds of war,
Oh, that from cobwebs, men's ideas were cleansed,
That things of evil might have their true names!
Then war would be called "hell" (too mild a
      term !)
And kings called "devils," and nobility,
(A gentle appellation would be "wolves,")
Could not exist to ever need a name !

September 1, 1882.

THE PATRIOT'S CHOICE.

What party of the free, to-day
 May claim the patriot's warm regard?
Is there a sun to light his way?
 Or is he from all light debarred?

Is there a compass, star or chart
 That he may trust and safely sail
To Freedom's happy port and mart,
 And shun the rocks and stem the gale?

"A good tree cannot choose but bear
 Good fruit" (the Bible plainly says,)
"The choicest fruit," (hear it declare)
 "Is mark of choicest tree always."

So we may take this chart and guide
 (The staff of age, the shield of youth)
And cross life's ocean deep and wide
 And reach the haven of all truth.

First, what's the tree? Where are the men
 That raised our ensign from the dust
Where it was trailed—restored again
 The Union—our immortal trust?

Have they a voice ?   And when they speak
Is their just mandate kindly heard ?
The men who fought, (the brave and meek)
What party hearkens to their word ?

It has my vote!   It is my choice
To stand with those who hear and heed
Their living, patriotic voice,
Who for the Union dared to bleed.

The people speak : " Remove the woe,
The curse that blights the hopes of all !
Strikes down our boys !"   O patriot know
What party hearkens to their call !

'Twill live while thus it represents
The progress of this lightning age;
'Twill live and give us Presidents,
Though "Stalwarts" bite the dust with
    rage.

The " Stalwart!"—type of dough-faced crew
That yielded to the "boss" demands
Of those who haughtily "withdrew"
To tear the Flag with bloody hands.

" Secession and State Rights!" the word
To hide their mercenary aims ;
They, hugging slavery, seized the sword;
The curse died out in blood and flames.

Old England--hypocrite and sneak!
Reached out her hand to overthrow
Our righteous government and wreak
Sweet vengeance on an ancient foe.

But she was foiled.   Again behold
Her coward form behind our door!
Armed *cap-a-pie* with British gold
The "Stalwart" is her paramour.

The wrath of man gives praise to God,
And out of evil good comes forth;
Our Fathers felt the tyrant's rod;
To Freedom, Tyranny gave birth.

Were not the people wide awake
To grasp the scoundrels by the throat,
The whiskey and gold "rings" would break
The rudder of the party boat!

When parties swerve from path of right,
And private interests seize control,
They fall before the people's might—
Thus perish every sordid soul!

Though war should follow, not a jot
Will patriots e'er budge from the track;
Remember the slave-holder's lot!
Remember the enfranchised black!

Next, what's the fruit?   Our land redeemed
From Slavery's black, all-blighting curse;

America, her flag esteemed—
Who follows now Secession's herse?

Honor to Lincoln and to Grant,
(The veterans that they represent—
Their fame's engraved on adamant)
Grant, General not President.

The end behold, of that dread strife,
The grandest government on earth!
Democracy clothed with new life—
And Liberty receives new birth!

How lenient! how kind1 how just!
May freemen now afford to be!
The olive branch extend—" distrust "
Write on the ensign of the free.

Distrust the men who dared to raise
Rebellious hands against the Flag;
Distrust the men who caught the craze
To cheer the hateful rebel rag.

Their just demands be quick to heed,
And be we toward them over kind—
And them as little children lead,
Yea, even to their faults be blind.

Yet, let them never rule the State,
And never hold the reins of power;
But let them ask and not dictate,
Ah, once they ruled, oh dreadful hour!

The Puritan gave us our laws,
　　The Puritan gave us our schools;
Ours still is Cromwell's "good old cause;"
　　Rave as we may, New England rules!

She ought to rule!　Her sons stand forth
　　The grandest, mightiest men of earth!
What is New England now?　The North!
　　Her ideas are our strength and worth!

And "Yankee" is a grand old name!
　　Yea, 'tis almost a hallowed word,—
The "Yankee Soldier,"—man of fame!
　　Too staunch for Jeff. and George the Third!

This is the fruit:　One word will say
　　All that a thousand words express—
The party lasts that will display
　　On high the glorious word " Progress."

"Go slow!"　The mandate of the wise ;
　　Go slow ; but on and always sure ;
Go slow; be ever on the rise!
　　On, on, up, up, toward heaven's bright
　　　door.

The party that sends to the rear
　　The dull, reactionary drones,
The party that will quickly hear
　　The voice of Progress and disowns

The knaves—the star-route thugs and
scamps—
Brings them to speedy punishment—
And e'en the gormandizing tramps
That lead astray our President—

(To save one leaky.lager-keg,
Hark! hear hoarse howls of rage and hate!
See bloated miscreants tear the Flag
And Constitution of the State!)

The party made of timber sound
(It comprehends a worthier sort
Of people, that with nerve profound
Enforce the laws) will hold the fort.

And to this party soon will haste
All patriots true of every name ;
The patriot will with patriots cast
His lot and shun the tents of shame.

October 10, 1882.

THE COPPERHEAD.

———o———

*"He got behind a mountain top
To hide himself from God."*—Old Song.

When blood of patriots was shed
The nation cursed the Copperhead,
Supposed she left the reptile dead;
    But is it dead,
    The Copperhead?

Our mothers shout, our wives rejoice
At Iowa's benignant voice:
But now we hear a hissing noise—
    Hark! Is it dead,
    The Copperhead?
A venom still the reptile hath,
All coiled up in the patriot's path:
Again we curse it in our wrath;
    It is not dead,
    The Copperhead!

How Iowa waked when Sumpter fell!
Recall the horrid rebel yell,
Our souls with indignation swell!
    Hissed at our dead,
    The Copperhead!

Again has Iowa awoke,
Hurled down Intemperance' demon yoke,
And quenched hell-fire ! Shall she revoke
    What she has said
    O Copperhead ?

Why show your fangs in this great hour ?
Think you to seize the reins of power ?
Think you our glorious flag to lower,
    By beer-bloats led
    Vile Copperhead ?

Loud was the boast : " Cotton is King !"
Who would rule now ? The Whiskey ring
But, mark me, Wrong's a feeble thing,
    A tender thread,
    Foul Copperhead !

Above us shines a glorious sun ;
For Iowa has her duty done,
A mighty victory she has won,
    Though snakes we dread
    Base Copperhead !

We struck down Slavery years ago ;
To-day we smite a viler foe,
The author of all human woe,—
    You've made your bed,
    Sleek Copperhead !

13

King Alcohol shall bite the dust
Smitten by Iowa's disgust.—
The Copperhead—but squirm it must—
    The devil fed
    The Copperhead !

The beast of the Apocalypse
O'er Iowa would bring eclipse ;
It kisses with its nauseous lips
    What erst it wed,
    The Copperhead !

August 18, 1882

LICENSE WRONG

———o———

Put it strong:
License wrong—
Hoist the sign :
"BEER AND WINE:"
Strike men down
In this town —
Curse the lives
Of their wives;
Make them slaves;
Dig their graves—
Poison Youth;
Murder Truth ;
Fill the air
With despair—
Put it strong :
License Wrong.

August, 1883.

AN "AMENDMENT" SONNET.

——()——

" If any man haul down the American Flag, shoot
him on the spot."—GEN. JOHN A. DIX, 1861.

These words have burnt their way into my heart!
  The Flag is emblem of rhe people's cause,
  Their righteous will expressed in righteous
    laws.
Brave Dix, thou 'dst make the accursed traitors
    smart
That trample on the Flag's great counterpart
  (The Constitution) with their forked paws!
  They belch foul treason from polluted maws,
And sell our country in the devil's mart;
Defy the verdict of the people's votes;
  Define the license "personal liberty"
  To drag our children to debauchery
And the society of beastial bloats.
Thy grim war order, Dix, we've not forgot;
  "Who lowers our ensign, shoot him on the
    spot."
Sept. 11, 1862.

TYRANNOUS ENGLAND.

——o——

A man named John McMahon, an evicted tenant, applied to the Board of Guardians for relief, when the following facts were elicited :

Chairman—I believe during the eviction a child of yours died.

Mr. McMahon—Yes, sir, a fine girl eighteen years old.

Mr. O'Brien—Was the agent there ?

Mr. McMahon—Yes, sir ; Mr. Bastable Hilliad was there. When my poor child heard that the Sheriff would come to turn us out of house and home, she being, ailing previously, became very bad ; and when we were put out, the snow falling thick and fast about us, I took the door off the hinges to shelter her, but the bailiffs pulled it away. My child died there, with nothing to protect her remains from the blast, but a little sheet.

Mr. McMahon, in reply to the Board, said that he had at present nine children beside his wife to support.

—Report of Meeting of Board of Guardians of Killarney, Ireland.

I execrate thee, England!   Thy tyranny
(More infamous than that of Muscovite
Or barbarous Turk, disgraceful to the age
That boasts of "progress" and "philanthropy,")
Must be o'erthrown!   All Christendom shall
    rise
Against thee—not with sword and needle-gun
And dynamite, that thou delightest to use
Against the Zulus—but with withering scorn;
Thy name, O England, shall be hissed by all—
Though speech and language are inadequate
To meet the horrors of thy cruelty ;
The Indian's scalping knife and tomahawk
Are kindness when compared to thy vile "laws"[
Yea, Nihilistic anarchy and war.
Nothing so cruel as thy "government ;"
Nothing so wicked as thy bailiffs are,
Acting obedient to thy lords' commands,
Thy boasted commons' and thy pampered
    queen's.

Sept. 11, 1882.

FORE-WARNED.

————o————

A very important case comes up for argument in the United States Supreme Court October 9th. It involves the constitutionality of the re-issue of greenbacks since the war.—*Associated Press Dispatch, Sept. 25th, 1883.*

Treason is rife to-day. The "Stalwart" breed
Have packed the Court with tools of Corporate
　　Greed—
Above the President the ermined crew,
Above the Congress and the people, too,
Now sit usurpers—tyrants, rank and vile,
Paid tools to enslave us to the British isle.
The trigger has been set; the deadfall see
Prepared to crush the life of Liberty !
The court, obedient to the "Stalwart" breed,
Obedient to the voice of British greed,
Will stab the greenback. It is doomed—and
　　lo !
We shall be plunged in a Hell of woe!
Columbia, see her writhe, see Freedom weep !'
Wake, patriots ! wake from Rip Van Winkle
　　sleep!
Arise and speak ; make known your sovereign
　　will—

The dart th it's thrown at you hurl back to
      kill!
Let " hari-kari" be the usurpers' lot
As when go vned Tyranny enslaved Dred
      Scott.

October 3d, 1883.

A SONNET

ON THE NULLIFICATION OF "CIVIL RIGHTS" BY THE
SUPREME TYRANNY

O Jefferson ! thy prophecy is true !
" *The Courts will overthrow our liberty ;*
They will become a hateful tyranny."
There is no villainy they dare not do ;
They re-establish caste, build up the few,
And re-enslave the millions we set free ;
They are a scab—a fatal leprosy—
A loathsome, rotten " eight-to-seven " crew,
Tyrants "supreme"—they nullify the laws.
O freemen! sound the tocsin of alarm !
Unfurl the ensign of the common cause ;
Put down usurpers with thy strong right
arm ;
Pull out the lion's teeth and clip his claws
Before he do Columbia fatal harm.

October 20th, 1883.

GRANTISM GARROTED.

———o———

CHICAGO, JUNE 2, 3, 4, 1880.

———o———

How the politicians revel!
  Bribed bulldozers,
  Loathsome leeches—
Vilest vermin of the devil!
  Third-term tories :
    Wranglers,
    Janglers,—
Hear their screeches!
    John Bull flunkeys,
    Monkeys,
      Braying donkeys—
Base be-gotten beasts of Belial,
  How they rant!
  Hark the slogan!
Conkling, Cameron and Logan
  Howl for Grant!

  The money ring
  By bribery rules—
  Conclave of fools,
  Gold is your King.

O. abject slaves !
O, shameless knaves!
Ye dig to-day your loathsome graves :
Ye sink so deep,
When Gabriel blows
'Twill not disturb your damned repose,
Your endless sleep!

June 3, 1880.

PASS THE HAT.

———o———

"We gave General Grant two terms of the Presidency and then dropped him to pass the rest of his days in poverty, with no opportunity to make a living. * * * *General Grant turned out to grass as his final reward."—*Chicago Tribune, Nov. 9th, 1879,*

"*A Colosus of ignorance.*"—CHARLES SUMNER.

Ulysses come to want!
        Pass the hat!
A "salary grabber" gaunt!
        Pass the hat!
Poor Grant " turned out to grass;"
        Pass the hat!
A pitiable ass!
        Pass the hat!
Starved bones led out to die;
        Pass the hat!
Ingratitude, "shoo fly!"
        Pass the hat!
A nickel will relieve—
        Pass the hat!
Poor starvling! thou shalt live!
        Pass the hat!

November, 1879

EPITAPHS

——o——

I.
ON A SORDID MILLER.

Here lie the bones of miller John—
Body rotted (soul had none)
He ground and ground and ground the poor;.
But now. thank God, he grinds no more.

July 15th, 1877.

II.
ON A MEMBER OF CONGRESS.

(Engraved with a pencil of chalk on his sarcophagus
of basswood.)

A big blockhead
Lies here, stone dead—
Gillette, Gillette—
Upset, upset.

August. 1880.

III.
ON A POLITICIAN..

Drop a tear
On Weaver's bier;
He defended the "Amendment" at last,
After it passed;
And he commended Prohibition
To perdition.

August 3, 1883.

PREFATORY

TO "LINES TO MR. KASSON,"

——o——

MY CABIN HOME SEPTEMBER 15, 1883

DEAR MR. KASSON ;—

I have carefully read your article in the *North American Review* of September, 1883, entitled, "Municipal Reform".

It seems to me that you take a wrong view of the matter. The evil is that the people *do not* govern—but designing "bosses" hoodwink and mislead the masses, and, prevent also, a fair expression of opinion by packing the primaries and "fixing things."

The doctrine of our fathers, as laid down by Jefferson in the Declaration of Independence, is the only true ground of political faith to be occupied by one who would be in line with progress, Reaction toward autocracy will never be maintained. It is my belief that you have departed from the faith of the fathers, and that the sentiments expressed in that article of yours will never be engrafted in our laws without a bloody struggle. I would die a thousand deaths before I would yield my assent to such principles.

While personally I desire to see you prosper, I will, nevertheless, combat the doctrines of your essay while I live, and I shall not scruple to speak with all plainness and boldness concerning them and you.

I understand full well that we have. in our country, a class of men anxious to subvert Democracy, and to establish, on the ruins of the Republic, an Empire. With your broad culture and deep insight into the

"hidden purposes" of the rich and powerful, and
your knowledge also of the ways and wants of the
poor toilers of America—belonging as you do by birth
to the ranks of the "producing class," I weep that
you have cho en to be an attorney for the "rich man"
in the new struggle for the rights of labor that is
now beginnirg. You have done well in your youth,
espousing the cause of the chattel slave—but now
comes the struggle to set free the "wage slave"—to
lift up the toiler out of the mire of degradation into
which he is sinking deeper and deeper by the fetters
of Monopoly being fastened upon his wrists and ank-
les, so that he cannot raise hand or foot to extricate
himself. I presume that young men will have to
come to the front and lift up the banner of reform.
We old Abolition workers, it seems, are worn out and
our vigor exhausted.

Very Respectfully Yours,
LEONARD BROWN.

I do not believe with Mr. Kasson that the
" ruinous principle to be expelled from the business management of our cities full of floating
voters is the rule which gives to a mere majority
of irresponsible numbers the right of control,
over the municipality ;" I do not believe that the
majority that so controls is a corrupt mob ;" I
do not believe that " the people who do not pay
are always ready to create debt against the people who must pay;" I do not believe it to be "a
sound principle, which would justify a limitation
of municipal suffrage to property owners and to
the payers of taxes ;" that is to say, I do not believe that as soon as the few have succeeded in
robbing the many of all property the many

should cease to have a voice in the government
of cities—that because a majority of the voters
of the city of Boston, for instance, are non-tax
payers, therefore a majority of the voters of
Boston ought to be disfranchised; and I do not
believe that "the control of the mere majority of
irresponsible numbers" is the "breeding nest of
municipal peculation, corruption, waste and ex-
travagance—the dark cavern of vicious politics,
the lying-in asylum of illegitimate politicians,
the nursery of corrupt practices."

The following "Associated Press Dispatch"
that I chance at this moment to see in a morning
paper, explains the cause of corruption of city
governments and shows also the remedy:

NASHVILLE, OCT. 12, 1883.
"The annual municipal election to-day, resulted in
an overwhelming victory for the citizen's reform ticket over the candidates for re-election of the old municipal regime.   The reform ticket is composed of blacks
and whites for the first time in the history of the
city. Tax-payers are jubilant over the defeat of
"boss" rule of the corrupt ward system."

" Boss" rule is what robs the city treasuries;
not the rule of the poor laborers, mechanics and
school-masters—poor whites or poor blacks
who live by daily toil, not the rule of the people
who do not pay taxes; for these are cheated out
of a voice under " boss" rule of the " corrupt
ward system." Vile "rings" of corrupt politicians "fixing" primaries govern these "boss"-

robbed cities. This is clearly shown in George
Walton Greene's " Facts About Caucus and
Primary" in the same number of the *North American Review*, in which Mr. Kasson's "Municipa
Reform" article appears. But the specific remedy is finally applied at Nashville. An appeal is
taken to the poor "colored men" for help, and
for the first time, in the history of that city, are
these poor people treated with justice and mag-
nanimity, and their manhood recognized. "The
tax-payers are jubilant over the result" of universal manhood suffrage and fair play for the
poor despised colored men.

Manifestly, the only true remedy for the evils
that afflict all governments—City, State and National, is to extend the elective franchise to all
adult citizens, male and female, native-born and
naturalized, white and black, rich and poor, and
thus make the public interests the business of
all men and all women, and the chief study of
the people in the home circle, support an independent press devoted to the interests of the
many and not bound with adamantine chains to
the chariot wheels of monopoly and jobbery and
corrupt "rings." There is no "corrupt mob" to
out-vote the masses, male and female. Let
these be not deceived and hood-winked and misled by designing demagogues, and the administration of the affairs of City, State and Nation will
be pure and satisfactory.

14

Mr. Kasson admits that in the most remarkable case in our annals this pillage of public funds was only revealed by an "*independent press* and punished by the *slow but firm uprising of an indignant community.*" This is a wonderful admission, pointing out, it appears to me, the only possible cure for the disorders Mr. Kasson complains of afflicting cities, and directing with index finger to correct "Municipal Reform" ☞ "AN INDEPENDENT PRESS"—"FIRM UPRISING OF AN INDIGNANT COMMUNITY." The "community" need not go so far as to "usurp the duties of the regular officers of the law," as it did in the case he mentions ; for the "community" is the only rightful appointer of "officers of the law." Let the "community" control and all is safe. Thieving politicians that usurp control through "boss" and "machine" management and who are not elected by a fair expression of the voice of the "community" must be put down. Let the people govern and all is well. But politicians elected to office by "tax-payers" alone would not necessarily be more "honest" than if elected by the "irresponsible majority." It does not make an official "honest" because elected to place by rich men, nor dishonest because elected by poor men, and party knaves may deceive the rich "few" as easily as they do the poor "many" —"daily personal association lulling suspicion" as well in the one case as in the other. Is it true

what Victor Hugo says? "Imagine everybody
governing! Can you fancy a city directed by
the men who built it? They are the team not the
coachmen. What a god-send is a rich man who
takes charge of everything! Surely he is generous
to take this trouble for us!" Perhaps there is
a little spark of irony in this, for Victor Hugo is
a Democrat. "It is," he says "the people who
are on-coming. I tell you it is MAN who as-
cends. Ah, this society is false. One day and
soon the true society will come. Then there
will be no more lords; there will be free, living
men. There will be no more wealth, there will
be abundance for the poor. There will be no
more masters, but there will be brothers. They
that toil shall have. This is the future. No
more prostration, no more abasement, no more
ignorance, no more wealth, no more beasts of
burden, no more courtiers, no more kings—but
LIGHT!"

Would not Mr. Kasson's logic end in making
city governments and all other governments auto-
cratic—upheld by and upholding a hateful plu-
tocracy, as two boards on end leaning together,
uphold each other—and would it not bring
back "divine right of kings?" Would there not
be a Dictator at Washington, supported by and
supporting the plutocrats of New York and Boston—agents of London "financiers," the Barings and Rothchilds—this Dictator appointing

" commissioners" to govern cities and States, as
Washington City and Utah Territory are tyran-
nized over to-day,—" model governments," according to Mr. Kasson's reasoning, Washington
City being governed by a board of three "commissioners," appointed by the President—(" Dictator")—and Utah Territory by a board of five
"commissioners," appointed by the President—
(" Dictator")! These issue "orders.'—or, in
other words, *make laws* for City and for Territory. This " commission" system is a damnable
tyranny, and history will so define it. And this
sort of government is preparing for all American
States and Cities, and Mr. Kasson's paper entitled " Municipal Reform" is, it seems to me, a
finger-board pointing the way to its speedy inauguration,   " Bosses" (corrupt politicians, who
have been fed at the public crib for a quarter of
a century, and petted by the people until they
have come to despise their masters, are evidently
plotting and planning the overthrow of democratic freedom on this continent. It is time the
patriots (toilers) of our country awaken from
their slumber of false security, and like Milton's
"strong   man armed," "shake their invincible
locks."

Mr. Kasson certainly fails to make clear a distinction between City and State governments.
The State does not " give " the people of a City
the right of self-government. " All power is in-

herent in the people." The City is a State, and
the earliest to adopt democratic governments,
Athens and Rome, for instance. The functions
of the City legislature are as important to the
the welfare of the people of a city, rich and poor,
as are the functions of the State legislature important to the welfare of the people of a State, rich and
poor. The State, I repeat, does not "give" the
City the right of self-government any more than
the Federal Government "gives" each State, admitted into the Union, the right of self-government. This right is God-given—a "Divine
right." Democratic government is peculiarly
well fitted to the wants of cities, and ever pre-
eminently satisfactory—calling out and develop-
ing the highest order of manhood. Democra-
cies alone produce great men. Let our cities
become more and more democratic; for the "irresponsible majority of numbers," that Mr. Kasson sneers at, will always do the right when they
know the right, When they do wrong it is when
they are misled. The poor non-tax-paying voters are not robbers. Poor men are ever the
most ready to give their lives an offering to save
their country's flag and liberty.

LINES TO MR. KASSON,

———o———

I.

O poor man's son! the rocks and stones and
    mountains of Vermont
Afforded hard and scanty fare—yea, you have
    suffered want!
Fatherless boy! kind Fortune smiled; we poor
    men of the West
Have been to you a tender nurse—have petted
    and caressed
Until we spoiled you—made you vain; and so it
    came to pass
That you "waxed fat and kicked," dear John,
    and "spake" like Baalam's ass.
You would have me, because I'm poor, "dis-
    franchised": Pay big rent—
Have bonds and gold or (like a dog) no voice in
    government;
Like Austria's cities let ours groan ; disfranchise
    all poor men—
All toilers; none must have a vote except the
    "*upper ten.*"
Is this the Tory gospel, John, that you've come
    home to preach ?

What have the millionaires, O, John, held out
within your reach?

Is this a bid for '84? Do you expect to bring

Yourself to be our John the First—our Emper-
or or King?

Is this the meaning of your speech? A bid for
something grand—

A bid for Wall Street now to make you tyrant
of this land?—

There is a plot (I know it, John,) deep-laid and
black and fell,

To break up Democratic rule—a plot hatched out
in hell;

But it will fail, and you, dear John, and every
schemer base,

Will meet your just reward and doom: discom-
fiture, disgrace.

Though peace is sweet and life is dear (I tell you
truth, dear John,)

Millions will die on battle-fields that Freedom
may live on,

Ere we, the poorest, lose our vote. 'Tis all we
have to give

Us hold upon a breath of air—the privilege to
live.

Our "one ewe lamb" is dear to us (the labor of
our hands),

Dear as the fruits of other's toil, to Lombard
Street brigands.

II.

The strong right arm of Labor wields the saber
  in the fight ;
The strong right arm of Labor will defend the
  toiler's right :
The strong right arm of Labor (let the rich man
  bear in mind)
Is the only ark of safety—more than "riches"
  to mankind ;
It is Labor th:t builds cities; Labor that pro-
  tects the home;
But the enemy of Labor stabbed the Gracchi of
  old Rome !
That enemy—the "rich man"—is determined to
  o,erthrow
To-day the friends of Labor as he stabbed them
  long ago!
But the day-star has arisen, and the night of
  gloom is past,
And now we cry "Eureka," for the morning
  dawns at last !
"I have found it! I have found it !" Labor now
  exulting cries ;
"I behold the promised morning; I behold the
  sun arise !
We are many ! we are mighty ! and the feeble
  ' Man of Sin'
He is fallen ! He is fallen ! and Christ's reign
  is ushered in,

Who has promised that the greatest shall be ser-
vant of the least,
And the poor he has invited to be present at the
feast,
And sweet Peace shall wed with Plenty and
Equality shall bless
The millions of all nations with the boon of hap-
piness."

October 11th, 1883.

OLD MEMORIES.

——o——

Read at the "Old Settlers'" Annual Picnic on the State Fair Grounds, near Des Moines, Iowa, August 16, 1883.

——o——

Well neighbors old, the day has come
  Dear friends again to see;
Long since we left our "Hosier" home,
  Or "Buckeye" (as't may be)—

Or "Wolverine" or "Yankee," too;
  "Corn-cracker," "Tuckey-hoe,"
Or "Sucker"—bade warm hearts adieu
  Oh, long, long years ago!

The oppressed came flocking o'er the sea
  Whence our forefathers fled—
From England, Ireland, Germany
  In myriads they sped—

"Entered" this lovely prairie land
  For better (not for worse);
Now let us grasp each friendly hand
  While old "yarns" we rehearse.

But neighbors old, how few remain
  Of first associates;
Their forms our memories retain :—
  My heart anticipates

A grand reunion soon, too soon;
  You see we have grown old;
We've passed life's morn; we've past its
    noon—
  The bell has often tolled!

Fewer and fewer meet each year
  To talk of days gone by—
Fewer and fewer shall appear;
  Our last hand-shake draws nigh.

But why, why talk in this sad strain?
  Here is no funeral, friends;
We are too happy to complain,
  And bright our day descends.

The evening has no clouds at all
  To early pioneers;
We're ready when the Lord shall call
  To join our old compeers.

Now bring the teeming baskets forth:
  To-day, with happy voice,
Within this "Garden of the Earth"
  We sing and we rejoice,

OLD MEMORIES.

Remembering still the good old ways—
  Recalling early scenes—
Privations of the trying days
  Of *hominy and greens.*

Oh, may the children still pursue
  The path their fathers trod;
Oh, may they ever live as true
  To Friendship and to God!

A SONNET

TO WILLIAM VAN DORN, MY DEAR DEPARTED FRIEND.

———o———

To thee, not as unto the dead, I speak,
   But as unto the living.   Art thou dead?
   Have life and friendship ceased with thee?   In-
      stead
They are intensified!   I do nct seek
Thee distant; but I feel thy presence near.
   O, Friend! 'tis but a day—a winter day—
And I'll have done my Earth-task, passed away,
And joined thee in that higher, happier sphere!
Me groundlings do not understand.   Thou did'st
   And lovedst me as one worthy thy regard.
Here, in this dreary atmosphere, amidst
   The virulent and gross, my lot is hard—
Maltreated, waylaid, mobbed by Envy's brood—
   Oh, may I bear my wrongs with fortitude!

November 10, 1883.

STANZAS

TO THE MEMORY OF HON, ROBT. W. STUBBS,

———o———

"POLK CITY. IOWA, Jan. 23, 1882,—We always feel
better when trying to do good than at any other time,
so let us ever be found trying to do all the good we
can."—R. W. Stubbs. (Writeen in his wife's Auto-
graph Album.

Heartrending scene! Wife, little ones
    Left suddenly to mourn,
Husband and father snatched away,
    Ah! never to return.

At post of glorious duty, Stubbs,
    Thy all thou didst defend;
Thy home, thy family, thy life,
    And bravely to the end.

How beautiful thy face in death!
    Pale, but serene and kind—
Reflection of thy blameless life
    And of thy happy mind.

A wreath of new-blown, forest flowers
    (Thy life's pure emblem) graced
Thy coffin, where by children's hands
    They lovingly were placed.

R. W. STUBBS.

For noble purpose thou didst live !
   Thou'dst have it understood
Thou ever foundst thy true delight
   In "trying to do good."

Can earth produce a truer soul,
   Sublimer, greater man
Than he who lives true to this line,
   "Do all the good you can?"

So passed the life of Robert Stubbs—
   For him, " to die was gain ;"
To country, friends and family
   Is sadly left the pain.

A SONNET

TO THE MEMORY OF ROBERT L. CLINGAN.

———o———

Clingan, how sudden was thy fall!—prepared
   And watchful, at thy post—a soldier true,
   You braved the danger as the bravest do,—
Drew forth thy weapon and the assassins dared.
Thou perfect pattern of a citizen—
   Benevolent devoted to the right,
   Philanthropic, "to do good" thy delight—
One of America's truest, noblest men ;
Thou wast cut off just in the prime of life:—
   Who may explain the mystery of the deed,
   And say why Providence had thus decreed
To afflict thy children and devoted wife
And bring such mighty woes upon our town,
Striking the best, hurling the purest down !

July 13, 1880.

RETROSPECT AND PROSPECT.

(1877.)

"I threw off," says Robert Burns, "six hundred copies of the first edition of my poems, of which I had got subscription for about three hundred and fifty copies. Who thinks the less of poor Burns now, that he took this method of publishing his poems? and who is not glad that he was not too proud to solicit subscriptions for his own work? The wise man "putteth his mouth in the dust if so be there may be hope."

But how vain and foolish to covet "success," unless one can leave behind him the memory of a life devoted to the good of others, as did the philanthropist John Howard. An anecdote is related of him, that when asked by an Austrian noble, what he thought of Austrian prisons, he replied : "The worst in all Germany, particularly as regards female prisoners ; and I recommend your countess to visit them personally as the best means of rectifying the abuses of their management." "I," said the astonished countess, "go into prisons!" The philanthropist replied : "Madam, remember that you are a woman yourself and must, like the most miserable female in a dungeon, inhabit a little piece of that earth from which you both sprang."

It was the Author's purpose, (when he gave the "copy" of this book to the printer) to have it include, in the following division, the principal patriotic pieces of *"Poems of the Prairies.* But its publication has been delayed by unforseen accidents until the time is now come when longer delay would be fatal to the Author's plans.

RETROSPECT AND PROSPECT.

——o——

SONNETS.

——o——

INSCRIBED TO THE FRIENDS OF CHILDREN.

I.

I now have reached my fortieth birth-day ;
  A braver battle few have fought than I ;
  Fearless have ever lived, fearless shall die,
Battling for truth and righteousness alway ;
Despising wealth, nor coveting long life ;
  Building a monument of worthy deeds ;
  Hating all shams and sanctities of creeds ;
Loving my children, faithful to my wife,—
And I've been blest beyond e'en richer men,—
  Fortune has smiled upon me graciously ;
  Domestic bliss has been vouchsafed to me ;
A feast of joy our humble board has been,
Our happy home, a cabin in the grove,
Seat of Contentment, Gratitude and Love.

II.

"Suffer the little ones to come to me,"
  The Master said, while wand'ring on the earth ;

' Forbid them not to climb upon my knee;
　My heavenly kingdom holds no higher worth.
　Where children do not gambol there is dearth
Of happiness.　Heaven, heaven would not be
If there the little ones we did not see,
　The air of heaven is res'nant with their mirth."
If not His words His meaning 't was the same.
　Of earthly joys the greatest is by far
　Where multitudes of little children are.
The joys of Croesus with his wealth were tame
Compared with joys of home: the warrior's glory,
The statesman's eloquence a sickening story.

III.

Mine are the joys of home and loving wife,
　And children, too, to love, a happy throng.
　Would I could celebrate in deathless song
What heaven has done to bless my humble life !
Ah, ye proud fools,　still hoard your ducats vain;
　At watering places strut like gaudy kings ;
　Ye butterflies of fashion, spread your wings ;
I hold your hollow joys in deep disdain ;
The fool's reward you surely shall obtain,
　Since Folly's shrine gets all your offerings.
I find at home far sweeter, purer joys;
My blooming wife; my romping girls and boys.
　From this fond circle ripest pleasure springs ;
For Love dwells here, and true love never cloys.

IV.

While babes are small what pleasure to supply
  Their little wants, to shield them in our arms.
  When they are happy how our bosom warms!
They look to us as we to Him on high.
To them the giver of each gracious gift,
  We feel the grandeur of our dizzy height;
  To give them happiness our chief delight.
Oh, if bereft of children, how bereft!
  A parent is the greatest of the great;
Nor Alexander in his grandest days
  Ever arose to loftier estate
Than to the parent is vouchsafed always.
Let us, then, rightly fill the honored station,
Give to our children noblest aspiration.

V.

But what if we are poor—our families large?
  Large families are preferable to small;
  'Tis but a little while we care for all;
The elder ones soon help us with our charge.
Given, then, of children say a half a score,
  'Tis easier to bring them up by far,
Than if you had a puny three or four;
  But industry must be the guiding star.
The poor man's children earn their daily bread;
  Nor do they need to work so over-hard
That they may not with hunger g o to bed;

Nor need you deem them (because poor) ill-
    starred.
Great riches are undoubtedly a curse,
They enervate the body—the soul worse.

VI.

A friend of mine once (driven to the wall)
From affluence *arose* to poverty.
    " No greater blessing ever fell to me,"
He said with tears: " My children, large and
    small,
Seem to correctly comprehend it all,
    And now betake themselves to industry ;
    Before were thriftless as they well could be.
My riches, then, I care not to recall ;
My sons will grow up to be better men,
    To thus rely upon their own strong arms;
    My daughters, too, 'twill give them truer
    charms
To work,—they sing as happy as the wren.
My mother, sir, could knit, and spin, and
    weave,
A better schooling than our schools now give."

VII.

Indeed, our college doors are all quite barred
    Against the children of the poor.   'tis so
    That, now, no other than the "Tally-ho"

May step into thy classic halls, Harvard.
But, since of Franklin still the name is heard,
   Think it no hardship, poor boy, to forego
   To learn at Yale or Harvard how to row.
The school where Lincoln studied is preferred,
And Johnson, Greeley, Clay and Faraday.
   Give me the school-room of the world, with
      God
To teach me, and throw colleges away,—
   The road to Fame is still an open road.
New England, of thy "culture" you may boast;
But of the mem'ry of thy Franklin most.

VIII.

Rounded and ripe as Attica of old
   When against Philip the great orator
   Thundered sublimely, deeply saddened for
The venality of Athens. Blackest mould
And rottenness we everywhere behold
   Among the rich—corrupted to the core!
Bright roses bloom with mildew covered o'er,
And priests and legislators worship gold.
But ever glorious her yeomanry;
   Like Putnam, loyal, patriotic, true;
Only in ranks of toiling poverty
"New England of the Fathers" yet we view,
Her churches trample down Equality;
Her colleges hug Aristocracy.

I heard a father boasting of his son,
  How he had risen to some honored place.
  What joy was beaming in that father's face
When speaking of the bays his boy had won!
Oh, let him boast ; yes, let the old man boast;
  I 'd rather be that father than to hold
  The highest rank on earth, and all the gold
Pizarro gathered and the Incas lost !
Let us embrace our children and be proud
  Of the inheritance we have received.
  Children are wealth, Oh, may it be believed,
Beyond that horded by the venal crowd.
Shame and disgrace to him—accursed his life—
That makes a barren mistress of his wife !

X.

The married " lady," (say, is God still just!)
  Of highest "culture" that the schools impart,
  Rebels against her nature and her heart !
What causes this decay, this cankering rust ?
If it be " culture " trample it in the dust !
  Go back to Nature; banish modern Art ;
  To books and schools and teachers cry"Depart!"
Yea, spit upon all learning with disgust.
Search out the hidden cancer ; show its cause ;
  Offshoot of wealth or pampered luxury
Or of bad education or bad laws ?

Destroy at once the deadly Upas tree!
How sad the home where children do not play,
'T is their sweet prattle drives life's gloom away.

XI.

What mighty int'rests are parents given!
    We act not for ourselves alone—but we
    Act for the good of our posterity—
Sublimest work, indeed, this side of Heaven!
We feel it is our duty now to leaven
    The world with temp'rance, truth and liberty,
    And have mankind embrace Christianity;
For children all, to make the chances even.
Let all men be compelled to give and do
    As if they loved their fellows as themselves,
Preventing thus the sefish, venal few
    From heaping all God's bounties on their
        shelves.
Arise our fervent prayer both night and morn:
"God, make it good for children to be born!"

XII.

But charity for them do not beseech;
    Loudly demand that children have their rights;
    The world belongs to them—all its delights;
Then hold not what is theirs out of their reach!
All children have the same God-given claim
    Upon the world, since all are equal born,

And naked all depart; then why not scorn
To rob the babes?   Riches are but a name.
More swinish than the swine, men sieze and
    hold
   Great heaps of rubbish that they cannot use,
   To starving infants nourishment refuse;
They die still holding fast their bags of gold!
Cruel and heathenish, they go to swell
The throng with Dives in the miser's Hell!

XIII.

How many orphan children crowd the streets,
   That have no friends, no home, no love, no
    care,
   And gain no pity of the millionaire!
He sleeps on down, and choicest viands eats.
Wrung from the hands of Labor, all his pelf,
   Through the sore cancer of monopolies,
   Now threatening all our cherished liberties,
Eating the life out of the Commonwealth!
Let us dam up these channels—stop the leaks;
   Build for the orphans homes of happiness—
   Lifting the helpless out of their distress
With money saved from grasp of pampered sneaks
That drive gay, prancing steeds as white as snow,
And cry in drunken chorus, "Tally-ho!"

XIV.

It must be done!   The time is near at hand
   When there will dawn a brighter, better day;

It will be said, " Old things have passed away,"
And Peace and Love triumph in every land ;
The "better way" the loving Master planned ;
    His coming little longer will delay ;
    Soon all the world His mandate shall obey,
And potentates will bow at His command.
Kings and aristocrats will cease to be ;
    Christ and the "common people" shall prevail—
The nations all a grand Fraternity—
    The proud " Republic of the World" we hail—
The glorious triumph of Democracy,
    When Wrong shall nevermore the right assail !

XV.

" The people's voice is voice of God" 'tis said—
    They do the right when e'er they know the
        right—
When they do wrong, it is when they're misled—
    And when they rule, they rule as in God's,
        sight.
    Dethrone the Kings and Mankind cease to
        fight ;
A brother's blood the people will not shed,
For they will all regard the Master then
    As erst they harkened to the words He spoke
    When He denounced the rich that bind the
        yoke,
Grievous to bear, upon their fellow men.
They " feared the people "—priest and scribe—
    for when

The Evil One directs envenomed stroke
Against the right, he never dares invoke
The multitude to aid him in his sin.

XVI.

It is the few that lead the world to evil.
    Preach to the people " honesty " 'twill do—
    'Twill never do to preach it to the few;
You would as well go preach it to the Devil.
The " rings " pool millions of corruption money—
    But did the people ever give a cent
    To bribe our Congress or our President?
You cannot say they ever gave one penny !
In dens and caverns of the dark earth, meet
    The agents of the gold monopoly,—
    Concert their schemes of fraud and robbery;
But they preach "honesty" upon the street !
The giant " rings " must first be overthrown
Before the car of Progress can move on.

XVII.

But now they read the writing on the wall ;
    Their doom's determined and the time is near
    When ends forever their corrupt career,
And, like Balshazzar's, great will be their fall ;
E'en now there's tumult in the palace hall ;
    The clanging spears and clashing shields they
        hear—
    And in the lofty citadel appear

Avenging swords that God will not recall
Before the poor His hand shall disenthrall,
  And little children shall have pitying ear ;
  For God is God, His veangence, Oh, severe
'Gainst those who make the helpless ones drink
    gall !
Their cries have reached Him and His strong
    right arm
Descends the whirlwind and avenging storm.

XVIII.

Woe to the tyrants that despoil our land !
  They cry "gold! gold!" raising great din·
    and clangor—
An Earthquake shakes the world with gentler
    hand
  Than the mad Tempest of a people's anger.
The Storm advances in grim garments dressed !
  The clouds, deep threatening, roll in wild
    commotion ;
Black Retribution, frowning in the West,
  Hurtles loud curses like the wrathful Ocean.
The storm-winds gather hoarseness overhead ;
  Louder and louder roars the bass-voiced thun-
    der.
The sky (its tongues of vengeance blazing red)
  Uncaves the ugly cyclone. Torn in sunder
Behold huge rocks and mountains ! In their
    dread

The Shylocks call for mountains to hide under.

XIX.

Away with caste!   The humblest man when
    free,
  Holds prouder rank in life than lord or king ;
  In all that marks the man (so poets sing)
The poor surpass the rich. How fervently
The laborer loves the children on his knee !
  His honest heart—an overflowing spring!
  He 'd freely give his life an offering
To save his country's flag and liberty.
He read of Marion when he was a boy ;
  He heard how heroes fought at Bunker Hill ;
His home, his wife, his children are his joy ;
  Hope swells his heart.   Perhaps his offspring
    will
Win wreaths of fame.   He says, "I toil for
    bread ;
My sons may strike for honor when I 'm dead."

XX.

FATHER.

His mind was fashioned in the woods of Maine,
  And of Ohio where Scioto flowed
  By the Wyandots' wigwams—there abode
His teachers and playfellows.   Him no chain
Could fetter ; and a stoical disdain

Was his of men's opinions, And he owed
All that he was to Nature and to God,
And to his blood that flowed of Scottish vein.
He read much—thought much. On him God
    bestowed
No ordinary gift of heart and brain.
Void of ambition—willing to remain
Down in the valley, and the muddy road—
Beloved by those who *knew* him—satisfied
That he was right (his heart *was* right) lived—
    died.

XXI.

MOTHER

O Mother could I but uprear to thee
    A monument immortal as thy love!
    Thou dwellest, mother, in the courts above.
From ills of life, from sorrow ever free.
Thou hadst not, mother, aught of vanity;
    But thou, a Christian woman, ever strove
    In holy walks and in the heavenly grove
To lead thy children ever lovingly;
Nor books perused, except the Book of God.
    To thee, in childhood, learning was denied;
But ever in the path of duty trod
    With holy zeal, and Jesus was thy guide;
Religion was a crown about thy brow;
Mother, thou art my guardian angel now.

TO CARPING CRITICS.

A SONNET.

———

I am unawed by all that fools may say ;
  Clearly in Faith's stereoscope I see
  My own America, the great and free,
In her munificence proudly repay
With wreath of fame, the Bird whose patriot lay
  Enshrines thy sacred name, sweet Liberty.
  It matters not how wise the carpers be ;
It matters not how lion–like they bray,
With hope undaunted, still unmoved I stand—
  Thou art, my country, worthy of my love ;
I look with pride upon my native land,
  And bow my knee to none but God above.
My harp is rough—a chip from Plymouth Rock ;
Its strings—the fiber of the " Charter Oak."

    May, 1865.

APPENDIX.

The following Occassional Lectures of the author's illustrate and emphasize the arguments already presented in his verses. They, therefore form an appropriate appendix to this volume, which aims to lay bare the wicked purposes of the secret enemies of American freedom and independence, to expose the treachery of false leaders and to point the way to the goal of practical equality.

It is to the patriotic reader the truths recorded in this work are confided. The venal soul that allows private interests to hold the mastery over his mind and heart, will not heed the appeals—however fervent —of disinterested patriotism.

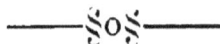

————§o§————

BOSTON, Sept. 12, 1881.

LEONARD BROWN :

DEAR SIR, I have received and read your essay on the "Vital Issue" with great interest. Its arguments are closely woven and very satisfactory, your facts marshalled in logical order and they march now on your reader with overwhelming power.

I rejoice to see these young minds in the ranks of a cause so momentous in its importance as that of the Nation's taking its currency into its own control.

Yours Respectfully,   WENDELL PHILLIPS.

OCCASIONAL LECTURES.

——o——

THE VITAL ISSUE:

BRITISH GOLD VERSUS AMERICAN LABOR, OR FRAUDS OF FINANCE.

A LECTURE
Delivered in Des Moines, Iowa, March 28, 1881.

Hoodwinking the masses is the last desperate resort of the "rich man" to hold labor in subjection in the United States, and pocket the fruits of toil through the manipulation of cash instead of lash. Cash is now king. How long. O Lord! how long before this king shall also be dethroned as was king Lash? May this cruel tyrant be put down by the potent ballot and may the bloody bullet be not again invoked in settling the strife between the many and the few, the toilers and the drones, the people and their plunderers!

I.—THE RESUMPTION FRAUD.

A bill was passed by our Congress in '69 to "strengthen the public credit" just at a time when our country stood in no more immediate need of credit than a well man does of medicine; but was (it is claimed) "rapidly paying off her bonded indebtedness." Why was not this "credit-strengthening act" passed during the war when our country was getting into debt and needed to have her credit strengthened? The fact is, the title of the bill is a fraud and a lie. The public credit has not been strengthened ; but the burden of debt has been more than quadrupled on the shoulders of the American people. The title of the bill should rather have been: "A bill to increase the burden of debt and to transfer the wealth from the hands of producing and laboring classes of the United States into the hands of the money-lenders—the Rothchilds of Europe and their agents in Wall street.

(1) The people are the public; the credit of the people is the public credit. Healthful national credit must stand on the same footing as that of the individuals of the nation. The credit of the people has been greatly weakened by a policy of government that has diminished the value of the products of labor and productive property upon which credit (national and individual) can alone be rightly founded. Any other foundation of credit is only enslavement of labor. The foundation being removed the superstructure, of course, falls to the ground. The foundation of the credit of the people is labor, the products of labor and real estate. Destroy their value and credit based upon their value is clearly overthrown. From 1862 to 1869 a farmer could borrow more money upon his prospective crop without giving a note of hand than he can borrow even now (it is not much amiss to say) upon this and all his personal property and real estate with notes and mortgage on top; for all productive property and labor and products of labor have had the bulk of the value squeezed out of them and this value has been squeezed into money (as Solon Chase expresses it) until the late secretary of the treasury, the Hon. John Sherman, proclaimed that the "purchasing power of the dollar has been increased by resumption sixty per cent."—which means that all productive property and labor and products of labor are sixty per cent. cheaper to-day, compared with money, than they were before resumption began in 1869, and therefore, the burden of the public debt is sixty per cent. greater. The immediate effect was to render labor and production unprofitable, as Mr. Sherman himself forewarned the people that it would do. Factories and farms not paying running expenses, the factories closed doors, the wheels of manufacturing stopped and the "operatives" were set adrift to wander as tramps, the nation losing during the period billions of dollars by the falling off of production; but farming had to go on with immense loss to the farmers as a class—mortgages on the farms the inevitable result, so that now, even in Iowa, the richest garden of the green

and bountiful earth, instead of there being as president Garfield says, " A prosperity without a parallel in our history," behold and consider the farms under mortgage, positively asserted by well informed persons, after careful inquiry and examination of records to be at the least calculation, *one-half!* This was not so ten years ago. The farmers were then out of debt, or, at least (to speak in homely phrase) the hole to get out of debt at was larger than the hole to get in debt at, but resumption opened wider the hole to get in debt at and plugged up the hole to get out of debt at. The wonderful prosperity " without a parallel in our history," (labor pretty generally employed, though strikes an every-day occurrence, tramps seen no more on our highways, a slight advance in the prices of farm products: but nothing like so high as in 1865, far below the point of deliverance for the debt-burdened farmer) has been brought about by only a moderate inflation of the currency, the result of an influx of gold from famine-stricken Europe and an increase of bank circulation, a wave that may at any moment subside and leave the ship of our present sham prosperity stranded high and dry upon the rocks. The usurers control in a great measure even now, in this country, the supply of currency, the national banks having nearly 350 million dollars of their paper afloat. When they find it necessary or expedient in order to advance their sordid and selfish schemes and robber designs, these banks withdraw their circulation. This they began to do the other day when interest on money immediately rose in New York City five hundred per cent. a panic, as on Black Friday, was imminent, caused by the sudden retirement of less than twenty million dollars national bank currency. Mr. Sherman, secretary of the treasury, at once hastened to the rescue of his imperiled " resumption," purchasing on the market, with greenbacks, twenty-five million dollars government bonds; thus a great financial crash, like that of 1873 was prevented. The people are between the jaws of a huge crocodile. There is nothing to hinder its crushing and grinding their bones to pieces between its teeth at any moment. This reptile is national banking and specie resumption.

It was evidently known to the money lenders of both hemispheres that resumption would force the people of the United States into excessive indebtedness, as it did the people of England after the long war, when the

number of land owners on the island of Britain was
reduced from 300 thousand to 30 thousand, and millions
of her people were made bankrupt and forced into ex-
ile to find new homes in the American wildernsss, as
all readers of history well know. Hence the trust and
loan agencies representing largely British capital, became as numerous in our country, and especially in the
rich West as green flies on a dead carcass in June or
July. Even in advance of the general demand for money here did the trust and loan agencies swarm upon
this doomed land. If the unfortunate farmer had not
money in bank when the resumption robbery began, he
was driven into debt to keep up necessary farm expenses (taxes, fencing, machinery, etc.) It is conceded that the mortgage on the farm may be traced, now
and then to bad management on the part of the individual farmer; but this cannot be put down as the rule,
that bad management on the part of the farmers puts
the farming class in debt; for the farmers are men of
at least, average good sense. Honest in their inten-
tions they are slow to believe in the dishonesty of others,
otherwise they could not have been so hoodwinked by
the money monopolists who now control legislation at
Washington, as to be led to acquiesce in a policy of
government so oppressive to the farming and producing interests.

The Old Testament history shows that, at one time,
the Jewish people "mortgaged their lands, vineyards
and houses that they might buy corn because of the
dearth." The reason why the people of our country
mortgaged their lands, vineyards and houses, was the
dearth of money produced intentionally and with "mal-
ice aforethought" by legislators, at the dictation of
European money lenders for the purpose of confiscat-
ing the estates of our people and giving them a bonus
to the owners of gold, thus opeinng the way here for
• bonanza farming" on an immense scale, and making
the farmers in this country hereafter renters, as in the
old world, and labor the obedient slave of capital.
This was no secret, even during the progress of contraction; but was openly avowed by the capitalists
through the leading metropolitan newspapers, both
Republican and Democratic—that give voice not to the
purposes and desires of the people, but only to those of
the "rich man." It must come, said the New York
Times (Republican) a change of ownership of the soil
and a creation of a class of land owners on the one

hand and of tenant farmers on the other—something similar to what has long existed in the older countries of Europe." And the New York *World* (Democratic) said: "The American laborer must make up his mind not to be so much better off than the European laborer. Men must be content to work for less wages. In this way the working man will be nearer that station in life to which it has pleased God to call him."

(2) The public credit is not strengthened; for, if another war were upon us, as in 1861, can any man say that the government credit would be better now than it was from 1861 to 1865?"

"If any, speak! for him have I offended." The money monopolists, it is evident, would do as they did before, combine to run the nation's credit down and to run the price of gold up so that they could reap another rich harvest from the misfortunes of our beloved country. They are only a banditti—and the sooner the people realize this truth the better. Let mankind combine against the money power as the money power have combined against mankind. Let the people protect themselves against their greatest enemy— the money sharks.

Bonds are increased in their market value because it requires for their payment sixty per cent. more of products than was originally contracted; and it is products that pay all debts. One dollar's worth of bond is worth almost two dollar's worth of wheat. The usurer gets almost twice as much for his bond as he is in justice and equity entitled to, of grain, pork and beef—also of lands, houses, beasts of burden, mills, factories, machinery, goods of every kind and description—books, paintings and every other handiwork, useful or ornamental. In proportion as labor is enslaved do the few find it easy to seize upon the products of labor. Is our country free to-day? No. Why not? Because millionaires are hatched out here. They are incubated only through slavery. Bad laws and bad institutions turn over to the few the proceeds of the labor of the many. Good laws and good institutions would prevent this. Capital is labor's products. It is perishable. Let labor cease and how long will capital remain? Ten years of universal idleness would render this world a waste. What now exists of labor's products will soon not be; so we will not quarrel about what now exists. What shall be produced by toil hereafter should belong to its creators, the toilers. This is our thesis. This we maintain is a reasonable demand. Let the laborer be not robbed of the fruits of his labor and all wealth will remain with the strong of arm who produce it. Stop "dividing up;" cease taking from the many by law and giving to the few, and the working bees will soon own and control all the honey, and the drones will be hurried outside the hive hungry. All is in a nutsh ll when it is remembered that capital is only labor's products, perishable, passing quickly away, to be renewed by toil, and that money is only a tool designed to aid production. The cheaper the money tool the better for producers, and it should, at least, cost them as little as it costs bankers—passing directly from the government to them without interest, as it does to the banks. It is possible to dam up the channels through which products flow out of the hands of the men who produce t em into the hands of the idlers the "tally ho" of eastern cities. These channels are the monopolies. Let "anti-monopoly" be the watch-word of all toilers and the day of labor's triumph draws nigh. The many serve the few through the wage system, land monopoly, corporate monopoly, and the bond system. The screws are turned by these giant powers and the wine is pressed out of the people's grapes for the exhileration and profit of the man in "purple and fine linen who fares sumptuously every day" and at whose gate Lazarus begs. The people are helpless as sheep before the shearer in the presence of the great engines of corporate tyranny, especially of the two thousand national banks that manipulate the bonds. Four per cent. brings as much of labor and products of labor now as a much larger per cent. did ten years ago (an end aimed at and secured by resumption and gold payment) and the principal of the bonds being made payable in "specie" by an *ex post facto* law (clearly unconstitutional) is enhanced in value beyond the ability of the people to pay for many years to come a continuous mortgage on the nation's wealth—sucking the life blood out of production for the benefit of a robber class destitute of patriotism, and given over to one passion alone insatiable avarice.

(3) What then is the nation's boasted credit to-day? Certainly not the funding of matured five and six per cent. bonds, by a "solemn contract" made payable in lawful money (greenbacks) into four per cent. thirty

year bonds, payable in gold or its equivalent? No,
not this.

" Harken that ye may the better hear!" It is the
stupendous lie that government has borrowed for
thirty years 175 million dollars gold of the European
syndicate at four per cent. annual interest. The government has "borrowed" not one dollar of gold. We
have indeed agreed to pay 385 million dollars gold for
175 million dollars greenbacks; and this, in truth, is
the whole sum of our boasted credit! "Let facts be
submitted to a candid world." Gold (175 million dollars) has been placed on deposit in the government
safe *on call*, the syndicate having it in their power as
all men know, to withdraw, in exchange for greenbacks "presented for redemption" every dollar of this
gold from the national treasury at any moment by a
click of the telegraph instrument. The late secretary
of the treasury, Mr. Sherman denominates greenbacks
"gold certificates." Wall street has this gold right
under its thumb. Greenbacks are advertised by government authority " redeemable in gold at the sub-
treasury in New York in sums of fifty dollars and
upwards." Will any man dare say that the money
power cannot command and present for redemption
175 million dollars greenbacks, when even the national banks profess to be able to retire instantaneously
200 million dollars of their circulation by *depositing
greenbacks in the United States Treasury to that
amount.* These bullionists act in concert the world
over. They are united as one man. Wall street is the
head-centre, the agency, in this country, of the syndicate of the old world. It is understood that the syndicate can and will remove this gold from the United
States treasury whenever they please to do so; and, it
is clear, that they will please to do so whenever they
lose control of our government. These millions of
gold will not remain on deposit in the national treasury, in all probability, ten years longer; for the people will certainly, ere then, awaken to see the situation and will as certainly throw off the yoke of their
foreign masters as our fathers did that of George III.
in 1776, establishing a legal-tender basis for money,
demonetizing gold and silver and wiping out the stupendous robbery denominated the national debt.

For the 175 million dollars gold placed by the syndicate on deposit in the government safe *on call* for
greenbacks, the government has given four per cent.

thirty year bonds, interest and principal payable in "specie," which Mr. Sherman defines to mean "gold or its equivalent."

Interest on these to maturity	$210,000,000
Face of bonds	175,000,000
Total	$385,000,000

gold paid by the people to "redeem" 175 million dollars greenbacks!

In the same fraudulent way the people are made to give in "gold or its equivalent" 175 million dollars for silver to displace for twenty years 50 million dollars fractional paper currency—three dollars and fifty cents gold equivalent for each dollar of paper money.

Bonds	$ 50,000,000
Int. 5 per cent. 30 years	75,000,000
Silver worn out in 20 years	50,000,000
Total	$175,000,000

The silver coin will be worn out and gone ten years before the bonds become due. As the holder of a sinecure in England is paid a large salary, or a "star route" contractor in our country "reaps where he has not sown," so do we rent at great cost imaginary silver. To keep 50 million dollars silver currency actually afloat until the thirty year bonds become due, will require

Bonded debt (additional)	$ 50,000,000
Int. 10 years "	25,000,000
Silver worn out "	25,000,000
Add previous expenditure	175,000,000
Total	$275,000,000

or five dollars and fifty cents "gold equivalent" for each dollar displaced of fractional paper money. The length of time silver coin in actual use as a currency is estimated to last is only twenty years, on a principle of reckoning similar to that which places the average life of man at thirty-six years. Some men, however, live to be a hundred years old and some silver coins are very ancient. Fifty million dollars silver coin to last a century for a currency will cost, on the Sherman plan

30 years bonds (5 issues 50 million dollars each,)	$250,000,000
Interest 150 years	375,000,000
Silver worn out in 100 years	250,000,000
Total	$875,000,000

to take the place of 50 million dollars fractional paper money, a better money than silver and that costs only the price of the paper and the printing—not so much as even the coinage of the silver—seventeen dollars and fifty cents "specie" (gold equivalent) for each dollar of paper money. This is a fair sample of the whole resumption cheat.

The government gives 210 million dollars bonus to European capitalists to induce them to deposit with our government 175 million dollars gold, to remain on deposit in the government safe just so long as the syndicate that deposits it pleases to allow and to be drawn out by them at their discretion in redemption of non-interest-bearing greenbacks at par, the government paying interest on the gold say, at least, twenty years after the syndicate has got it all back in their own vaults in exchange for greenbacks, 385 million dollars gold paid for 175 million dollars greenbacks—two dollars and twenty cents gold for each dollar greenback money.

At one time during the war, the patriotic bullion owners bid one dollar gold for two dollars and eighty-five cents, greenbacks, investing in greenbacks at that price, they said, "to make some monish." Now the grateful government "resumes" giving the bullion owners two dollars and twenty cents gold for each of at least 175 million dollars greenbacks "to strengthen the public credit."

II—THE NATIONAL BANKING FRAUD.

Let us now look at the national banking fraud.

The notes of these banks are said to be "redeemable." This saying is a lie. They are declared by law "receivable at par in all parts of the United States in payment of all taxes and excises and all other dues to the United States except duties on imports, and also for all salaries and other debts and demands owing by the United States to individuals, corporations and associations within the United States, except interest on public debt." And the statute also expressly declares these notes "money." Why was this endorsement given them by the government? Being thus endorsed, declared to be "money," and forced into circulation paid out to certain creditors of the nation ["honest," must we say, "to pay those creditors national bank 'money;'" "dishonest" to pay bond owners greenbacks!] and received in payment of public dues by

the authority of law, renders national bank bills
practically identical as money with greenbacks in
which they are pretended to be redeemable. National bank bills are no more redeemable than are silver
and gold. They are inter-changeable at par for other
forms of money. Trade dollars are not thus interchangeable because not legal tender. It is clearly
not optional with government, "individuals, corporations, and associations" to "receive" national bank
bills or not when presented or tendered in payment of
taxes and debts as the law directs. They are, by law,
compelled to receive and not refuse them. Law lays
down a rule binding every day, every hour, every
minute and every second until repealed. Therefore
until the statute (speaking the nation's voice repeal-
ing this robber law) says "refusable," the bank bills
must circulate as fiat money, and never return upon
the issuer. It is a huge sham to talk of one money
being redeemable in another money -the one being
made as good by legal endorsement as the other. Legal-tender and *quasi* legal tender may be interchangeable, but not redeemable, interchangeableness being
the result of par value, not par value the result of interchangeableness. No man will ever be so idiotic as
to present a national bank bill for "redemption" in
greenbacks with the expectation of obtaining a better money thereby while the bank bill continues "receivable" for taxes, salaries, etc: The authors of this
measure to conceal their selfish purpose evised a cunning heat, procuring congress to place upon the bank
bills the word " receivable" instead of the word "legal
tender." Worthless non-interest-bearing bank notes--
the credit of private corporations, they had government
endorse and make practically legal-tender under cover
of the word receivable." "Grave doubts" have never
been entertained by the national bankers, nor by their
accredited agents in the presidential chair (it would
seem) of the power of congress to do this. It is (we
must conclude) in their opinion "constitutional" for
congress to enact that national bank bills "shall be receivable at par in all parts of the United States in payment of all taxes and excises and all other dues to the
United States, except duties on imports and also for
all salaries and other debts and demands owing by the
United States to individuals, corporations and associations within the United States except interest on public debt." But to bestow precisely this same, tax-pay-

ing and debt-paying quality and power on greenbacks, the credit of the government "grave doubts are entertained whether it is warranted by the constitution," say they. The national banking corporations have issued their ukase and three successive presidents of the United States in the role of heralds have proclaimed it: "*The greenback must be destroyed.*" Then will the money lenders have the people completely in their power and all business under a deadfall. The banking and credit or class may spring the trigger, crush all industries and bankrupt society at pleasure gathering all the property of the debtor class into their possession.

The endorsement of government clearly monetizes the national bank bills, equalizes them with greenbacks in money quality for the payments named in the law and for all other payments, since no one will refuse that "money" which the government of his country accepts, without it may be the national bankers themselves who, having this license, will use it when it shall be to their interest to do so. Who will present an axe to be redeemed in another axe no better than the one to be redeemed? The axes might be interchangeable if equally good, it being then indifferent which axe one had to work with,—interchangeable because equally good, not equally good because interchangeable. A distinction with a marked difference. Nick badly one of the axes, leaving the other sharp, and they are no longer interchangeable the one for the other indifferently. The sharp axe will be taken by the workmen every time and the dull axe left behind. Nick the greenback deprive it of legal tender quality, as President Garfield asks Congress to do, and no man will take greenbacks when bank bills can be had that have the word "receivable" stamped upon them by law —take away "receivable" from bank bills, as the people should compel their servants—the law makers at Washington—immediately to do, and no one will take bank bills when greenbacks marked "legal-tender" can be obtained.

But let Congress attempt to demonetize the national bank bills and the national bankers will protest against it loudly, unless the greenbacks are demonetized at the same time. They will not oppose the demonetization of the national bank bills after the greenbacks have all been destroyed: for they have so declared in resolution at Saratoga; since, to deprive the

people of all debt-paying, tax-paying paper money
would render them still more powerless and dependent upon usurers. Nothing but specie paying taxes and
debts, and the banks cornering the specie they would
hold the people tightly in hand and well under the
yoke. Bank paper would still circulate; for the people must have a paper currency and "wild cat" is
preferable to no paper money at all. Legal tender paper afloat, bank notes could not by any means have
been palmed upon the people during the war but for
their endorsement by government. This is the reason
why "receivable" was printed on the bills. Government endorsement was essential to the bank note then,
because the greenback existed and while the greenback
continues to exist it is essential still. Bank paper cannot survive and float beside the greenback a day without being *quasi* legal tender—a greenback in disguise,
but a thief and a robber in fact and in deed. The reason why old style bank notes ever floated as a currency
is, clearly, the superiority of paper money over metal
money in convenience. The people were willing to
take risks and receive bank paper solely because of the
inconvenience of handling specie. It was a price paid
for convenient money that every dollar of wild-cat paper did not hasten immediately back to the banks for
redemption in coin. Nobody wanted coin if paper
could be had that was passable, and nobody wants
coin to-day, as Mr. Sherman himself admits. The
bond-owners are clamoring for the demonetization of
the greenbacks so that bank bills may be the only paper money of our country and the lords and gods of the
United States be forever the national bankers. Says
the *New York Mercantile Journal*: "The national
bank managers insist upon retaining power to regulate
the volume of the currency at their pleasure, and without any restriction from the laws under which banks
are organized. Twenty years ago the government
could have as logically surrendered its capital to the
rebels, as Congress can now surrender this power to
the banks or to any particular class of its citizens."
Did not the banks threaten the government and the
nation the other day with a contraction of the currency
that would destroy all business, and did not President
Hayes get down on his coward knees to them and veto
the refunding bill at their dictation? and does not President Garfield say: "The refunding of the national
debt at a low rate of interest should be accomplished

without compelling the withdrawal of the national bank notes and thus disturbing the business of the country?"—"Compelling!"—the banks hold over the heads of the people the threat of "retiring their circulation" to *compel them* to yield to the wicked demands of soulless corporations, mad as were the slave buyers before the war and as determined to rule or ruin. But each and every national bank bill would be " retired from circulation" by the people themselves "pass to the bourne whence no traveler returns"—be spurned as they ought to be now under our feet, if they were not "receivable" for public dues, etc., but depended sor value on redeemability in legal-tender paper money. Having no superiority over greenbacks in convenience (as old style bank paper had over specie) and being no longer "receivable," bank bills would not be in any demand when greenbacks could be obtained. National bank bills are practically an " irredeemable" currency, there being no difference in their nature from greenbacks in a legal sense—even exempt from taxation as a form of "government credits"—same as greenbacks. The points of difference are these: their tremendous expensiveness to the people and the sham pretense of being an " innocent note payable in greenbacks on demand." They are a lie, a cheat, a wholesale robbery of the people, a confiscation (at one swoop) of 350 million dollars of the nation's wealth and its bestowal gratis on the bond owning class—and this last statement will bear repeating until public attention is awakened to the enormity of the wrong.

It is worthy of special note that while bank bills are practically legal tender in payment of public dues, salaries of officials, as postmasters, etc. for soldiers pay and pensions of disabled "boys in blue" and their widows and orphans—for wages of all laborers employed on public works—carpenters, masons, hod-carriers, etc., —to canal, railroad and ship companies for transportation of troops, munitions of war and carrying the mails—to manufacturing companies in payment for powder, balls, pistols, guns, cannons, and all other war implements and material—to merchants for clothing, and to farmers for provisions for army and navy to ship builders in payment for monitors and other ships of war—yet they are not "receivable" by the bankers themselves as a class for what the people owe them. And the government, too, is choked off from paying the national bankers in heir own

"money" the interest on the very bonds that are the
basis of the banking fraud.   Each banker is obliged to
accept only his own individual currency from the people and not national bank bills in general—and from
the government not even his own individual bank notes
as interest on bonds, which " shall be paid in coin."
Who dictated the passage of this despicable act, ex-
empting the national banking class from the necessity
of taking bank " money" and forcing it on government
and individuals?   The people never dictated the passage of any such preposterous law; but only the brazen-
faced national bankers themselves. The national bankers have been presented a bonus of 350 million dollars
tax-paying, debt-paying "money"—a virtual confiscation, (I again affirm) of 350 million dollars of the people's property and the giving of the same gratis to a
class of men able to live without being thus supported
as paupers by lavish taxation and sweeping robbery of
the producing class. Giving away the checks for property is the same thing in effect as giving away the
property itself that the checks will buy— a wholesale
confiscation (let us ever bear in mind) of 350 million
dollars of the people's property and its bestowal gratis
on the bond owning class—"communism," indeed of
the most hateful type; for it is robbing the poor to
give to the rich. Give me the checks for all the property of the nation and all the property of the nation is
mine, as when I have a sheriff's deed for your farm it
is mine. Let prices rise or fall it is no matter. I can
command all things for sale. Let the farmer be deluded
with an apparent high price for his grain, pork and
beef, in consequence of an inflation of bank bills—it is
only a delusion -the grain, and pork and beef are the
bankers who have received as a gratuity from government the checks that must command the surplus
products and the labor of the land. Inflation of bank
bills and consequent advanced prices of labor and
products, are no sign of prosperity of producers and
laborers as a class, but mark only the issuance by g v-
ernment gratuitously to bond owners of so many more
checks for property and labor—the confiscation of so
much more of the wealth of the country and its bestowal gratis on the bond-owning class. The bond owners
have only to present the checks that cost them nothing
and walk off with the property. Let the government
legalize counterfeiting as it has legalized national
banking and it would be no greater but only the very

same wrong to labor. And let it give into the hands
of a few counterfeiters the monopoly of issuing an unlimited amount of counterfeit paper money, the government endorsing this paper as it does national bank
bills, (which are, in fact, only counterfeit money legalized) let these monopolists issue at once 350 million
dollars of this sham "money" made a good as gold by
legal endorsement– same as national bank notes are.
Times w ll, of course, become flush, because of the
abundance of this counterfeit currency; and shallow
observers and interested liars and deceivers of the
people will gloat over the "wonderful prosperity" of
the country, as they do now. But the fact will ever
remain incontrovertable, as it is to day, under national banking, that the ownership of 350 million dollars
worth of property thus passes from the many to the few
––from the people to the counterfeiters. This is national banking (legalized counterfeiting) and its results
as seen to-day in our country. What a tremendous
advantage this robber system gives British capital over
American labor! British capitalists through their
agents establish and control the principal money corporations in America. It is British capital under specie basis and national banking that moves and controls
through Wall street, all the great operations of business and exchange on this continent. By giving up
the legal-tender greenback, we abdicate power, surrender sovereignty, become vassals and slaves of England – paying tribute to her moneyed aristocracy beyond all that is exacted by her from India, Africa,
Australia, Canada, and all her other colonies and pos-
sessions, and far beyond the wildest dreams and ex-
pectations of George III, and the fears that led our
fathers into the war of the Revolution––the annual
drain on American production for interest alone even
now, being (as will be more fully shown before the
close of this lecture) not less than 1,300 million dollars!
An English writer lately said: "The large capital of
England is the most essential weapon now remaining
by which our [England's] supremacy can be maintained." And the *London Economist* adds: "When
the United States debt is paid off it will, in effect be
a subtraction from the profits of European capital equal
to an income tax of three shillings in the pound."
How true are the words of Mr. Winder, who, in his
testimony before the monetary commission of the

2*

Forty-fifth Congress, said: "The power of a creditor country over the currency, interest and welfare of a largely debtor country with convertible currency, is more searching, absolute and despotic than that of any tyrant that has ever plundered the people. And he further adds: "But the great, and transcendent wrong (and most absurd violation of every principle of justice and political economy) was the change of payment of the bonds from greenbacks to coin. But it was of a piece with all the rest of the financial policy of our government, which seems to have been (as most assuredly it was) as wholly in favor of foreign interests and against American, as though our administration had been conducted exclusively by foreign cabinets."

The Old World has gold that has been, thousands of years, accumulating in the vaults of her banks through usury and the plundering of weak nations by force of arms in the interest of the lords "of cash." The New World has products that spring almost spontaneously from her virgin soil. It is evidently the cunning and hateful purpose of the Old World bullionists to absorb (or steal) the products of the New World through interest paid by us to them, for a thing we do not need, and really cannot use, *i. e., gold.* Suppose Mr. Sherman did, indeed, purchase in good faith with the four per cent thirty year bonds 175 million dollars British gold now in the treasury, intending it to be coined into currency to circulate in the channels of business, here instead of legal tender greenbacks, until worn out—a very few years—not over fifteen; for gold being softer, wears out more readily than silver- the cost to the people will be a clean loss of

Bonded debt to be paid	$175,000,000
Interest 30 years	210,000,000
Gold coin worn out	175,000,000
Total	$560,000,000

for the sake of having in circulation for fifteen years 175 million dollars gold coin in the place of 175 million dollars greenbacks. To keep this amount of gold currency in the channels of business here for thirty years on the Sherman plan, as above, will cost our people 1,120 million dollars; and for one hundred years 3,700 million dollars a constant outflow of 37 million dollars yearly tribute to England, while greenbacks would cost comparatively nothing, saving to our industries nearly every dollar of this vast sum, which must be paid to European capitalists in our surplus products, wheat, corn, pork, beef, cotton and wool, etc., at gold prices—lower and lower as gold becomes scarcer and scarcer. * * * * Gold and silver must be "monetized" by legal enactment to be valid money same as paper, which if furnished the people by the government after the plan of 1723, so highly approved by Dr. Franklin, would be a source of revenue to our country.

But paper money is now, has been for many years and ever will be practically the only money of business. Let this be no longer issued as a loan without interest by the government to bondowners. National banking should be at once suppressed. If under this system we are not compelled as "individuals, corporations and associations" to borrow directly the foreigner's gold, we are compelled to borrow national bank bills, issued by our government gratis to the agents of British capitalists, who have invested their gold in American bonds. How completely, then, the national banking system and specie basis bring us into dependence upon foreign bullion owners for money both paper and specie! We exchange government bonds for bullion to be coined into specie, and these same bonds are then made the basis of national banking—ninety per cent of their face value being returned to the bond purchaser by the government, in national bank money made as good as greenbacks by government endorsement—a free gift to tne bondowners— one hundred thousand dollars, four, five or six per cent bonds, costing the banker only ten thousand dollars. Upon this small investment he draws from the production of our country four thousand, five thousand or six thousand dollars yearly interest.

Rather let the law say to every working man in America "Deposit your earnings in the money-order postoffice, receive from government four per cent annual interest on the same for thirty years, take back immediately from government ninety per cent in money as good as that you deposit—on the same terms that bondowners are given ninety per cent of the face value of their bonds in tax-paying, debt-paying "money." Such appreciative attention to the interests of the toilers by the government would be a great boon to the industrious, going far to preserve in the hands of the working people the wealth produced by them. If the government must pay interest, let it be paid to American workers to stimulate production and aid producers, and not to British capitalists and their agents to be used by them to break down our government, as those capitalists attempted to do by openly assisting the South in the late war, for which England was compelled to make restitution to the United States for damages of sixteen and one-half millions of dollars, British capitalists are our enemies to-day, as they were during our civil strife. British aristocracy is the unrelenting foe of American Democracy.

Why should not the toiler have the right to deposit even his ten dollars and draw upon it four per cent annual interest for thirty years, receiving also immediately from government nine dollars of currency, if the bondowner, is allowed on his one hundred thousand dollars invested in bonds four per cent annual interest for thirty years and a bonus of ninety thousand dollars legal paper "money?" Is not the ten dollars of the earnings of an American laborer as deserving of a bonus of nine dollars and four per cent annual interest for thirty years, as the one hundred thousand dollars of bondowners, money, got by usury, is of a bonus of ninety thousand dollars and four per cent annual interest for thirty years? Let the toilers of our country demand equal rights under our laws with foreign capitalists and their Tory agents here that manipulate the government to sustain the national banking swindle.

Then (to show more clearly the superior possibilities and "advantage" of national banking even, on a small scale) the working man might, with a capital of only twenty dollars, deposit in the money-order postoffice ten dollars, receive back nine, deposit ten again, receive back nine, and going on in this way until he has not a ten to deposit, he would have the government indebted to him one hundred and ten dollars, and yet have remaining nine of his original twenty dollars capital. This investment of only eleven dollars, would bring him four dollars and forty cents per annum interest, forty per cent or in thirty years one hundred and thirty-two dollars, drawn from the national government. Figures do not lie. This is an epitome of the national banking system. At the end of twenty years the banker has received from government eighty thousand dollars interest on a ten thousand dollar loan—40 pr. ct. pr. annum. Every 4 per cent bond held as the basis of national banking, pays the banker forty per cent per annum, while his bank charter lasts, every five per cent, fifty, and every six per cent, sixty, for one hundred thousand dollars in bonds costs him only ten thousand dollars—the ninety per cent tax-paying, debt-paying money returned being practically a free gift to the banker from the government. To lend the banker,(or any man,) money for twenty years without interest is, in effect, to make him a present of the money, to say nothing of the banker's having his loan renewed by getting his bank "rechartered" at the end of the twenty years, which he confidently expects to do, and certainly will do, if the people do not again take control of the government and prevent it, as they did when they elected old "Hickory" Jackson, of blessed memory, President. Truly the national banking system gives the capitalists an unlimited power over the people, of taxation and extortion—a power greater than our government itself possesses, that, in theory, cannot tax the people without their consent (though in practice it often does.) These corporations are the absolute masters of the American people to-day. O that we could say in reverbant tones, awakening a slumbering nation: *They shall not be so to-morrow!* They can bankrupt and make a tramp of every business man in the United States in thirty days; and they will do it whenever they deem it to their interest. They threaten it now, if not obeyed by the recreant old-party leaders, who are, at this moment, in greater terror of the banks han the Czar is of the Nihilists. Let the national banks suddenly retire their circulation 200 million dollars, as they have threatened to do, if not obeyed by the government, and ruin will sweep through this land, devouring all business as the flames devoured Chicago. Public indignation, rising to sublime intensity as it did in the North when Beauregard opened fire on Sumter, would bury the rotten leaders out of sight. Our country to-day is Prometheus,

"Chained to the cold rocks of Mount Caucasus"

the national banking corporations are

"The vulture at his vitals;"

corrupt party leaders, Vulcan, who forged the chains that bind our country. The "links of the lame Lemnean" are indeed "festering" in her flesh!

If the laws would only declare farmers' notes without interest secured by first mortgage on productive lands (the notes covering say ninety per cent legal valuation of taxable land —same per cent of credit as is allowed capitalists on non-taxable bonds) "receivable at par in all parts of the United States in payment of all taxes and excise and all other dues to to the United States, except duties on imports and also for all salaries and other debts and demands owing by the United States to individuals, corporations and associations within the United States except interest on public debt," how soon would the farmers be free from the burden of usury? These notes being thus ' monetized" by the endorsement of the general government and put afloat by the farmers in all parts of the Union most distant from the homes of the persons issuing them (as bank notes are) they would never come back to the farmers for redemption any more than bank notes come back to bankers for redemption. Let them float for twenty years the same as bank notes; then at the end of that time " recharter" them to float without interest or redemption for a second twenty years, and then again for a third, and so on *ad infinitem* same as bankers propose for their currency, as will be presently shown. Then might we sing.

"The independent farmer!" The farmer would be king. He ought to be. Agriculture should be fostered by legislation. It is the supreme interest. But, it appears that the farmers, in this rich and productive country, have become the abject slaves of gold monopolists of the old world reduced to this condition by the financial policy of our government foreign bondowners dictating the laws British oligarchy governing America.

But President Garfield asks congress to do something for the farmers of our country. "The interests of agriculture" he says in his inaugural address, deserve more attention from government than they have yet received. The farms of the United States afford homes and employment for more than one half our people and furnish much the largest part of all our exports. As the government lights our coasts for the protection of mariners and the benefit of our commerce, so it should give to the tillers of the soil the *lights of practical science and experience!* Money is of supreme interest to American farmers as well as to foreign owners of American bonds. Give our farmers the same benefits of financial legislation as are given by our government to the British owners of our bonds, (or a tithe of those benefits) and our farmers could then hold their grain, pork and beef in spite of European combinations, and America could set her own prices on her own products. Europe would be compelled to get down on her knees to us, since the old world must have these products or starve. The new must feed the old, worn-out world. Which ought to be king, bread or gold? Which is of greater importance to mankind? When we need gold it hides, as during our war. When we do not need it 'tis forced on us, as to-day. Ought gold fix the price of bread, or bread fix the price of gold? Let gold fix the price of bread, we are slaves. Let bread fix the price of gold, we are freemen. Right here lies the heart of the issue between hard money and soft—between gold and greenbacks. The man that stands over me and says what I shall have and must accept for my products and my work is my master and I his slave. America is the slave of England because of specie basis. Gold means our enslavement; greenbacks our freedom and independence. With legal-tender paper money filling all the channels of business here Europe has nothing that America is obliged to buy. This accounts for the great interest John Bull takes in American monetary affairs. The greenback is our second Declaration of Independence. Let us defend and perpetuate it with "our lives, our fortunes and our sacred honor" if need be. "Independence now; independence forever," being the sentiment of every true patriot heart as it was the "living sentiment and the dying sentiment of John Adams. If the old world were to sink under the sea a thousand fathoms deep it would not make a ripple on the placid ocean of our prosperity *if we cut loose from gold.* We can live and prosper conquering a gigantic rebellion while gold hides its infamous head. But for our government to legislate value right out of our lands, labor and products and legislate that value right into British gold right out of everything we do possess and right into the very thing (gold) we do not possess, and even threatening, at the same time to destroy the Lincoln greenback, the savior of our nation's life, the source of our prosperity, "a present help in every time of need," and then buying gold bullion of the foreigner with interest-bearing bonds and returning to the bondowner, gratis, ninety per cent of the face value of these bonds in tax-paying, debt-paying "money better than gold itself, because more convenient, and making gold the "measure of all values" here—is not this getting down voluntarily on our knees to Europe? Who is the Benedict Arnold that has thus surrendered our country, to the foreign enemy? British capitalists cornering the gold and controlling the amount of money in our country, both specie and paper, do now even to-day, fix the prices of our products, lands and labor, holding us as dependents and slaves. Is any man so blinded by party spirit he does not see this?

Can any man fail to see that all the millions of dollars paid by the people of this country to money lenders for interest would be saved to the American producers if the government gave the same favorable endorsement to well-secured, non-interest-bearing notes of farmers, manufacturers, merchants, mechanics and laborers as it does to the non-interest bearing notes of bond-owners? Bank notes (so called) perform the functions of money; so would these as well under a system that could be made plain and practical in a bill not half so long and intricate as the national bank act—which was made so on purpose, no doubt, to deceive the people whom it was desired to defraud and rob.

Bank bills are recognized as "money" by the laws—then they are given as a bonus to bond-owners for twenty years—the length of time their bank charters last. At the expiration of the first twenty years, if the bondowners still control the government as they do now, the charters will be renewed for another period of twenty years and, at the end of that time, again for another period of twenty years, and thus on and on *in perpetuo*, a debt without interest never to be paid as long as foreign bullion owners and national bankers control our government and the national banking law remains unrepealed—stolen property to be held until the people recover it from the thieves.

Besides the 350 million dollar steal, the national bankers have received from our government in interest on the 400 million dollars, bonds, the "basis" of the banking fraud 20 million dollars per annum, amounting in twenty years to 4C0 million dollars, a sum that would have been saved to American producers, if the bonds had been "cut up in little bits of

paper" and put afloat as greenbacks. Not only would
the 400 million dollars interest have been thus saved,
but the 400 million dollars bonded debt, also, floating
among our people as greenbacks would have been a
perpetual blessing—not a debt to be paid but an instrument to promote the prosperity of our country
forever.

The American people have lost then in twenty years
through the national banking swindle

Interest on 5 per cent bonds.............$400,000,000
Bonds.................................... 400,000,000
Paper money gratuity.................... 350,000,000

    Total............................$1,150,000,000
All this vast sum has been worse than thrown away
—enriching as it does the few, increasing their power
to oppress the people and corrupt the officials of government and impoverishing the many innocent victims.

Let us look at the loss already figured in round
numbers far below the aggregate as the figures before
given do not include the 28 million dollars annual interest paid by the people to the banks for the privilege of using bank notes as money. The figures should
show:
Bonus paid on gold deposit fraud........$ 210,000,000
Bonds for said sham...................... 175,000,000
Silver swindle to displace fraction pa-
  per currency for 20 years.............. 175,000,000
National bank swindle.................. 1,150,000,000
Add 20 years int. paid for bank notes 8
  per cent........................... 560,000,000

    Gives total.......................$2,270,000,000
But the national banks made not less than forty per
cent profit in purchasing the bonds at a discount with
depreciated greenbacks in the beginning. Forty per
cent of 400 million dollars equals 160 million dollars.
Thus have the people of the United States been gulled
out of 2,430 million dollars, a sum vastly larger than
the indemnity levied by Germany upon France at the
close of the Franco-Prussian war (and these figures
show but a tithe of the loss to our industries already,
by this baneful foreign system of finance) robbed of
this vast amount by the European Rothchilds and
their agents, the national banking syndicate that
holds its annual congress at Saratoga New York, the

United States government enforcing their robber decrees.

Do not the national bankers pay taxes? Not a tithe of what producers pay—not a hundredth part of what is given them as a gratuity by the government do the national bankers ever return to the federal treasury. "One per cent of their issue" pays not the printing of their bills and bonds—costing the national banker not so much to issue his notes as money as it does a counterfeiter to print counterfeit bills.

If national banking is so profitable why do private banks exist?

Because private banking has some advantages over national banking for men of moderate capital:

1st. The private banker has the lone and sole management of his business.

2d. The private banker has the benefit of all deposits, discounts, etc., and has not to share profits with associates in business as in national banking, where "the big fish eat up the little fish."

When a national bank breaks is it not compelled to redeem its notes? If finally for any cause a national bank is compelled to surrender its charter (these banks never do or can break unless in stock gambling or other outside speculations foreign to the banking business,) the government redeems the outstanding bank notes in gold bought of John Bull with interest-bearing bonds, thus making our bond system perpetual, and repays the bank every dollar it has ever really paid for the bond—ten per cent of its face value. When banks "retire their circulation" they only exchange with the government paper money for gold paid finally on the bond. In short the national banking system is the climax of fraud and wrong, the fruitful source of corruption and betrayal of public trusts. The national bank and railroad corporations now control two branches of the federal government —the legislative and executive. The judicial branch of the government will be a pliant tool in their hands before 1884 ; for the new judges will be of their choosing—e. g.—*Stanley Mathews.'*

III—BOND-AND-NOTE-AND-MORTGAGE-INFLATION-FRAUD.

The people are taught by the capitalists through the bought-up newspaper press that "an inflation of greenbacks is a great evil." On the contrary, the exact truth is, such an inflation operates as a bankrupt law to free the multitude of laborers and producing men from debt—a great public blessing. But there is, indeed, an inflation that is a woeful curse to our country—an inflation of bonds, notes and mortgages in the pockets of money-lenders. Such an inflation, has unfortunately fallen upon our fair land to-day—a blight upon all legitimate business- the death and destruction of all prosperity—a sweeping confiscation of the property of the many and its seizure by the few.

Money may be made so plentiful (if issued by the government to the people in general as is now done to bondowners in particular) as to put all laboring and producing men practically out of debt, or it may be so contracted as to throw all this class hopelessly into debt. The rule will work both ways. We have seen its workings. Time was when money was abundant. Then agriculture and labor and production of all kinds was profitable. Then the laborer could, in a little while, from the profits of his labor pay for a comfortable home. But there came a change with contraction and resumption and an odious inflation of notes and mortgages took place. Prosperity now poured in upon money-lenders and adversity overwhelmed laborers and producing men. The tramp was hatched out. Laws became oppressive and men were imprisoned for no crime but that of asking a crust of bread. A standing army of eleven thousand troops—nine regiments of infantry, one of cavalry and one of artillery was enlisted for five years in Iowa. What for? To hasten the period of "stronger government," the foreclosure of mortgages and the transfer of the landed property from the hands of the many into the hands of the few—from the people to the money-lenders.

When the greenbacks are "inflated" the people make large profits from agriculture--one or two crops often paying for a good farm—they make large profits from all sorts of productive labor. When greenbacks are contracted and bank bills, bonds, notes and mortgages are inflated, the profits that before flowed to the producers and laborers now flow into the coffers of money-lenders. All that labor has accumulated the money-lenders seize upon and pocket. It is only a question as to which kind of inflation shall prevail—inflation of money in the pockets of the people or inllation of evidences of debt against the people in the pockets of usurers? Withdraw the money and the people are overburdened with debt. Says Mr. Jones, in his excellent book, "Money is Power?" "The effort of credit to fill the vacuum caused by the retirement of 1,000 million dollars from the business world, explains the mystery of the burden of debt which has pressed so hard upon the country." Under an inflation of nearly 2,000 million dollars of currency in the pockets of the many at the close of the war, the people rejoiced ; now, under a tremendous inflation of 26,000 million dollars bonds, notes and mortgages against the production of the United States in the pockets of the few, the people mourn. This estimate agrees with the statement presented in the work above named :

National debt.........................$ 2,000,000,000
State, municipal and railroad......... 4,000,000,000
Debts of 630,000 traders, manufactur-
  ers estimated by the monetary com-
  sion.................................. 13,000,000,000
Banks, mining and other companies..   7,000,000,000
    Total ....$ 26,000,000,000

Interest at only five per cent becomes an annual drain on our country's production of 1,300 million dollars, and at eight per cent of 2,080 million dollars, requiring the labor of ten millions of men at seventeen dollars and thirty-three and one-third cents per month, working all the time, from the beginning of the year to the end, in sunshine and storm, to pay it—the labor of all the voters of the United States! If saved to our workers language would fail to express the happiness it would bring them; but robbed of it what misery, murders, suicides, snd untold horrors are left in its stead!

Contraction of the currency at the dictation and command of foregn bullionists brought upon us this immense load of debt. The overthrow of the national banking system—the wiping out of the bond swindle—the complete demonetization of both gold and silver—and the devotion of American law-makers to the interests of their own country and countrymen as they are now devoted to the interests of for.ign bullionists, would insure a supply of "lawful money" (greenbacks) that would free us from the burden. Bankers and money-lenders do not object to "inflation ' if it means bonds, notes, mortgages and even "money" in their pockets. They only object to inflation in the pockets of the people. They feel precisely the same interest in the people that wolves do in sheep. In a late number of the *New York Herald* it is proclaimed that "an inflation of real money is as injurious as an inflation of sham money." But bondowners do not object to an inflation of bank bills. How many millions of dollars have been added to bank note circulation since 1879! Money must flow out to the people through the channels of the banks and loan agencies not to be "injurious" in the estimation of money-lenders. Any amount of money among the people, got afloat on first mortgage loans, bringing large interest to the lenders and enslaving the borrowers is "healthful." Otherwise any sort of money in the pockets of the people is "bad." Let the people be prostrate at the feet of the money power—as dependent on usurers for money as a sucking calf is upon its dam for milk and all is satisfactory to the enemy in his war against greenbacks and labor. The only meaning of the finance question then is: Who shall govern America—the Rothchilds and their agents, or the American people? If the people do not control the paramount interest of finance they do not control the government. We cannot say ours is a government of the people, if the most important public interest is under the management and control of an irresponsible few. Let us cease to depend on the few for money, and the many may hold and control what they produce by labor. Demonetize gold and silver and let legal tender paper flow out from the people to the people through the government of the people, and we have the highest blessing that can be secured—independence. Who should have the direction of the financial affairs of a farm, the owner of the farm or the irresponsible hired hands? Uncle Sam purposes controlling and directing in every respect the finances of his big farm. The banks are doing practically the work of most important public officials in issuing and controlling the volume of the nation's currency—a most vital trust and without being in any way responsible to the public. They are only responsible to the bullion-owners of the Old World. Whoever dictates the financial legislation of a people is practically dictator of that people. It is through their financial policy alone that nations are enslaved—and the end of all enslavement is financial—the obtaining the products

of labor without giving the producers an equivalent
—"wrenching from the hard hands of peasants" the
fruits of their sweat and toil by force or by fraud. It
is fraud we have to deal with now; but force i threatened and is not far off—if the people by vigorous
thinking, disinterested, acting for the public weal and
independent voting, do not hurl tyrant capital from
his throne and crown labor king. Everlasting chains
and slavery are in reserve for the people of the United States—lab r mangled, crushed, bleeding and torn
—unless the engin that is now plunging rapidly on toward this frightful Ashtabula is immediately re-
versed. Plainly then the question is: "Sha l the people control this government for the greatest good of
the greatest number, or sh ll the money-lenders control it and use it as an engine of robbery and oppression of the masses—establishing on the ruins of the
republic a stronger government of money and bayonets

THE CONCLUSION.

This momentous political crisis is forced upon us by
the money power (stronger than the slave power of
old) involving all that was at issue in the revolution-
ary struggle- -the independence of America and the
welfare of the toiling millions for many decades, and
even centuries, to come. Let us know no North, no
South, no East, no West, but one united commonwealth, the toilers of all sections, of every color and
race, our beloved countrymen, and stand once more as
our fathers st od, for the "inalinable rights of man,"
for the preservation of popular liberty and equality
before it is too late, before the nation has passed beyond the reach of the patriot arm to save.

"What constitutes a State?
Not high raised battlement and labored mound
Thick wall and moated gate—
Not cities proud with spires and turrets crowned;
Not bays and broad-armed ports
Where laughing at the storm rich navies ride;
Not starred and spangled courts
Where low-browed baseness wafts perfume to pride
No; MEN, high minded men,
With powers as far above dull brutes endued
In forest break and den
As beasts excel cold rocks and brambles rude—
Men who their duties know
And know their rights and knowing dare maintain
Prevent the long-aimed blow
And crush the tyrant while they rend the chain—
These constitute a state
And sovereign law that state's collected will
O'er thrones and globes elate
Sits empress crowning good, repressing ill.'

PART II.—THE TRIUMPH OF LABOR-- A GLANCE FROM 1876 TO 1976.

A CENTENNIAL LECTURE WRITTEN IN 1876.

1876 finds our country overwh lmed with debt—impoverished by bad legislation—the government corrupt, and a dread apprehension on the minds of the people of further betrayal by officials in high places. But the people are true--the love of liberty is not dead—is not extinguished in the minds of the laborers of our country. The reaction towards aristocracy and despotism, that has taken place, will be but temporary.

> "Freedom's battle once begun
> Bequeathed from bleeding sire o son,
> T ough often baffled 's ever won."

The battle begun by our fathers for human equality will continue. Let me, then, recount the real glories of to-day and anticipate the good in store for us, and the world that the coming century will bring.

One hundred years ago who could anticipate the progress of to-day? The progress of the century has been mainly in the direction of mechanical inventions. Old times produced greater poets; greater orators; greater painters; greater sculptors; greater architects --but in the direction of labor-saving inventions, the century has leaped forward a thousand years--has eclipsed all the past. Thus man has grown to be a giant in physical strength--and the world must soon be subdued, and th rough places made smoo'h—the hills brought low. Soon there will be no desert places—no barren regions. Nor is this imaginary, Saharah is an ancient sea-bottom and rich--wanting only wat r to be extremely fertile. By boring a few hundre et in depth, it is said, we strike abundance of water below the sea level--filtered into and through porous rocks- and the average cost of an artesian well that raises four hundred gallons of water per minute is fifteen hundred dollars. In such a climate as that of Northern Africa, where two crops a year may be produced--a land of dates and figs and olives—by turning the money expended in guns and munitions of war and feeding and clothing the three millions of European soldiers in arms to day, and their labor, also, in the direction of subduing the desert--how long before it would be reclaimed and grand cities be seen where all was once desolation and drifting sands —and Saharah smile and blossom as the rose and fields of bright grain cover the plains from Morocco to Soudan? There is not a spot of earth but will one day afford a happy dwelling place for man, while the ocean itself will be crowded with floating palaces, the homes of myriad sons and daughters of the sea. Man will be master of the physical elements. He will not longer look up to the clouds for rain and sit trembling fearful of drouth and famine. Machinery will water the farms—the moisture will be lifted from below. Man will be supreme on earth and may proclaim

"I am monarch of all I survey.
I have tamed the lightning; the deep is obedient to me; earth serves me; Nature bows before me and pours out her treasures at my feet unfailingly."

The physical world is an exact mirror of the world of mind. Observe the wilderness of nature—the barren deserts unreclaimed, and you see a true picture of the human mind that (as the world shall be redeemed to culture and beautiful gardens bloom where now thorns and briars only grow) shall also put on her garments of love—and selfish cease to prey upon the weak, as the lion upon the lamb—but we may hope for the fulfillment of the prophesy that the lion and lamb shall lie down together and a little child shall lead them. I want to believe that the coming century will see selfishness dethroned.

I do not expect that greater inventions than steam navigation and the magnetic telegraph will ever be made, for there evidently is a limit in the direction of great inventions. During the next hundred years, what is already found out and is now rudely put in operation, will be so perfected that the resources of the earth will be brought forth for the use of men with far less physical labor than now—the unification

of the world realized—no important city or place on
earth remaining isolated—all joined together by railroads and telegraphs—mankind one family of love—
Africa redeemed—the whistle of the locomotive heard
on the shores of Lake Nyanza—manners, customs and
institutions of all nations conformed to the Christian
law of love- and the people have gained the mastery
over all governments—a general disarmament be
brought about—all disputes between nations settled
by a world's congress—a union of all effected the
proudest banner that shall wave from the dome of the
centennial building at Philadelphia—the city of broth-
erly love—in the year 1976, will be, I trust, the flag of
the UNITED STATES OF THE WORLD.

It is the idea of the equality of men that is working
in modern history for the emancipation of labor and
the redemption of the world from the domination of
kings, of wealth and of priestly power. May we not
anticipate the overthrow of all kingly governments
in Europe ere the next centennial? There will then
be a disbandment of her armies. The people, entirely
free, will vote to maintain no standing armies. The
word "reciprocity" will be emblazoned on the world's
banner--"Do unto all as we would have them do unto
us." Peace is to the interest of the people—the few
reap advantage from wars. The few who reaped
material advantage from the war of '61 are our millionaires of to-day, who send agents to congress to control legislation by bribery and corruption. The people enlightened will never go to war. The republics
of Greece and Rome were warlike; the free bands
of Indians inhabiting America were engaged in continual wars; yet I maintain that no enlightened *Christian* people will engage in aggressive war. As soon
as the fundamental Christian law "Love thy fellow-
man as thyself" has been crystalized in the customs,
laws and institutions and governments of all *Christian*
nations, wars must cease. This idea of the supremacy
of the law of love was not fully accepted among even
the most highly cultured of the nations of old; but
all European nations now believe it to be the bounden
duty of ma i in his relations to his fellow-man, to en-
tertain the same affection for him as for himself.
Though this is universally admitted by Christian peoples, yet the idea has not been crystalized in institutions, laws, and governments very generally; but, on

3*

the contrary, the *corner stone* of all seems to be *selfishness*. It is true, corporations have been instituted for benevolent purposes and for mutual aid. Hospitals for foundlings and for orphans have been established by these corporations and by individuals—sisters of charity sent to nurse the sick—and there are Free Mason and Odd Fellow fraternities. Now we are beginning to have *state* asylums for the blind, the deaf, the insane, etc ,—and we have Soldiers' Orphans' Homes supported by the state. But the great advance of the coming century will be in this direction. All destitute and orphan children will be gathered into the arms of the loving commonwealth. The youth must be cared for and properly educated before crime can be put an end to. As long as the cities are full of little ragged street *Arabs* sleeping in goods-boxes by night and running uncontrolled by day, under no guardianship of fatherly hands—with no wholesome food to eat; no good books to read; no schoolmasters to instruct them—just so long will the prisons be crowded with criminals. May we not hope that before the next centennial pleasant homes will be provided for all destitute and orphan children?

Go with me to a beautiful village in Iowa in the year 1976. This town belongs to men who have been convicted of crime, and are here put under guardianship, as if they were children—and are given work to do and wages for doing it. They work a part of the day and another part they devote to mental culture. The state aims only to build up those men into good citizens worthy of freedom, and resorts to kindly means for the acomplishment of this purpose. This penitentiary is a *reform school*, nor are the convicts subjected to any harsh usage. They are, it is true, deprived of liberty, dear to every man, are declared "minors in law" and are kept under restraint; but they are surrounded by elevating and reformatory influences. It is the aim of the state to teach them self-respect. They are, therefore, shown the utmost kindness. Society is thus protected and the vicious class given honorable employment and are compelled to earn their living by honest labor. There is no discomfort here. The inmates of this reform institution converse with each other and are as free as hired laborers to-day. Indeed this village is an asylum for the morally weak, where they resort to be strengthened—a retreat, a home. Punishments have been abolished,

The state I claim has no right to punish men for crime; but only the right to bring them under guardianship and restraint; the right to settle them in one spot, depriving them of the liberty of emigration and there giving them remunerative employment and teachers and books and hope and courage and ambition and public spirit.

The "signs of the times" point, also, to the speedy overthrow, even in Great Britiain, of that accursed institution, land monopoly, the most unjust and oppressive monopoly that has descended to us from the barbarous age. It is the *essential* evil. Remove this and all other forms of oppression die. Conceive of a State in which no man is allowed, by the laws or customs or institutions of society, to own more land than a convenient homestead, more than will yield him subsistence by being carefully tilled by his own hands, more than, say forty, eighty or one hundred and sixty acres of productive land; and you at once have before your mind a society of equals, a society in which poverty is unknown, in which luxury is unknown and its consequent immorality and enervation of mind and body, a hardy race of freedom-loving men and women as in Switzerland.

What obstacles are in the way of the removal of this monopoly to-day? None whatever. It is altogether in the hands of the state. It is a monopoly sustained only by law, and that, too, *unjust* law. It is sustained through no principle of right, but only by unrighteousness and barbarity. These beautiful plains are the common inheritance of all. Through untold ages the soil has been accumulating its productiveness for the benefit of man. This inheritance belongs to all alike, as the water and the air. Embrace, O, Commonwealth, in thy protecting arms these lands as homesteads for thy children! Save them from being seized upon by robbers, as in Europe!

John Stuart Mill says: "When the sacredness of property is talked of it should always be remembered that this sacredness does not belong in the same degree to landed property. No man made the land: it is the original inheritance of all the species. * * If the State is at liberty to treat the possessors of land as public functionaries, it is only going one step further to say it is at liberty to discard them. The claim of the land owners is altogether subordinate to the general policy of the State. The principle of property gives them no rigkt to the land; but only right to compensation for whatever portion of their interest in the land it may be the policy of the State to deprive them of."

He further says : "War among nations and discord among individuals grow with the growth of monopoly in land. The more perfect its consolidation the greater must be the inequalities of society, and the more must those who labor be made to suffer in the distribution between the people and the State."

The time will come, and that speedily, I sincerely hope and trust, when the laws will not be partial— will not confer upon men the license to seize upon and hold what is not theirs by natural right. "Land," as Mill says, "is the original inheritance of the whole species." By what right may a few seize upon this inheritance of all? By the ancient law of barbarity— the law of *force*. This law must be done away. RIGHT must rule. The natural rights of man, must be enforced by the laws. Let the few hold their millions of gold and silver, and countless diamonds and rubies and pearls. We want none of these. They are baubles—play-things for children. But let these rich people own no more land than other men; take nothing from them, but pay them for their surplus land in money—as the people before the Rebellion would have been willing to pay the slave-lords for their slaves. Yet it is a serious question whether it is just to pay a man for that which he has no right to. And what right had the slave-master to his slave?— and what right has any man to a monopoly of the land?

Can human law give one a right to what is not his by divine law? The vast mine of wealth opened to the world by machinery belongs to all mankind. The advantages and benefits of all inventions should be made general—should shorten the hours of labor for every man, woman and child, until the amount of exertion necessary for subsistance would be but slight. The strife among men then will be not for wealth, but for intellectual grandeur; for building up the Angelic in man; for calling out the immortal beauties of mind and skill. The reward fame—renown. T e grandest man will be he who has developed the grandest soul; the loftiest mind; the noblest heart—who has devised the greatest good for his neighbors—instituted the best schools—the most com-

fortable homes for orphans and widows, and the aged
and the helpless—has been the greatest benefactor of
his race. This, then, is the problem for legislation to
solve: How may the surplus wealth of the earth,
produced in such abundance by human skill and inventions, be prevented from being taken possession of
by the few—how may it be distributed through the
arteries of society for the benifit of all? This problem will, I trust, be solved before the centennial of
1976. Millions will not then be calling for employment and bread. All men will belong to the laboring
class then. The class that now lives above manual
labor will be abolished. Every man will be compelled
to earn his living who is physically able. That there
is a fixed purpose in the minds of the producers to
bring about this reform is manifest from the following article of the platform adopted by the farmers
and working men in convention at Indianapolis, Indiana, June 10, 1874. They say:

"We hold that all able-bodied, intelligent persons
should contribute to the common stock, by useful industry, a sum or quantity equal to their own support,
and legislation should tend, as far as possible, to the
equitable distributation of surplus products."

Manufactories are public servants; but under the
present system of monopolies the servant is the master. A mill is built with private capital. The miller,
for sixty pounds of wheat, gives thirty pounds of
flour, keeping one-half the weight of the grain.
Would any one contend that it were good policy to allow horses and oxen, sheep and hogs to pasture on the
grain-fields? How much would be trampled under
foot and wasted if the farmer did not reap and thresh
his grain and give to each of his dumb servants a due
portion; but let them range at will through the fields.
The mills, factories, railroads,etc., are public servants,
just as horses and cattle are for the service of men.
But the people do not as yet say what the mills, factories, railroads, etc., shall be fed; but literally turn
them out loose into their fields to destroy, waste and
trample down the grain, having gorged themselves until their sides are swollen out to an undue bigness.

Co-operation is the remedy—each individual con-
tributing a small portion to a general fund, and this
general fund be the feeder, or moving force of all
manufacturing, mining, banking, commercial, transportation, and all other interests now controlled by

private capital. How will this fund be raised? In
just the same manner as the school fund is raised. A
tax is levied upon the property of a neighborhood to
build a school house. In like manner let a tax be
levied to build mills, factories, etc. (Already railroads are built in this way; but the people who build
them do not own or control them, but give them a
bonus to private corporations for private profit.) Take
(for example) four townships embracing a section of
country twelve miles square and contrining 144 square
miles. Each square mile (if there was no waste land)
might include eight farms of eighty acres each or
1,152 farms in all. Each farm paying twenty dollars
tax would give a fund of $23,040, which would build a
good flouring mill, or a woolen manufactory; or a
plow and machine shop; or a grain elevator; or a pork-
packing establishment. One hundred dollars tax on
on each eighty in a section of twelve miles square
would build all these and (I would add) a narrow
guage railroad besides across the section.

It is by individuals and private corporations controlling these necessary interests that wealth concen-
trates in the hands of the few, and millionaires are
evolved among us and swim in the midst of American society, as did the prehistoric monster reptiles
among the smaller fishes, devouring them at pleasure.
But if the state or people become the master or owner
of all public establishments, railroads,etc., the wealth
will remain with the laboring classes that produce it,
and equality be preserved. All are created equal, and
that equality should be enforced and maintained. All
should work, and all should enjoy the fruits of their
labor. Machinery will have become such a vast help
in producing sufficient for all, that each man will
need to labor but a small part of his time. Three
hours will be a day's work. Books and study and
mental culture, and " to do good " the chief end and
aim and *religion* and ambition of universal man. All
nature will be subject to man, and man subject to the
law of God. The community will enforce this law.
The few that would seize upon and hold the surplus
wealth of the world by *force*—that is, by what is
termed " legal right "—the same right by which the
slave-lords held their four millions of blacks in bondage, these few will have to allow the commonwealth
to hold what justly belongs to the commonwealth—
the surplus products of labor—will have to conform

to the law of God, unjust "legal right" being taken
away, as has been the right to hold slaves in our
country.

Are not private corporations more injurious than
beneficial to the public? Are not all European nations to-day combatting the giant corporation known
as the church? Has it not bound in fetters of iron
and trodden down the weak for a thousand years? It
was instituted for a benevolent purpose—to save men
from sin—to do the highest and holiest work. If the
church, as a *political corporation*, has proven the
greatest enemy of men, why should not the people
look with distrust upon all close corporations that
they cannot directly control? Railroad, insurance,
and banking corporations exercise vast influence for
evil. The sole object of their management is the ac--
cumulation of wealth--not the public good—and the
public suffers in proportion, as they are uncontrolled
by legislation; and those corporations exert vast influence over legislation. For instance, we adopted
England's money-order system. Why, have we not
adopted her system of Postal Savings Banks? President Grant advised Congress to adopt this other excellent reform; but the banking corporations of our
country said "No." Money being the object of those
corporations, they favor only that legislation that
pours money into their coffers. They know nothing
but venality; they look not beyond the boundary of
their own circle, or "ring." The corporation becomes
a petty state, and claims all the patriotism of those
whose monied interests are bound up in it—all outside interests are alien. All corporations are in their
very nature anti-democratic. Monopolies flourish
best under arbitary governments. There is, then, a
constant tendency to autocracy in a country cursed as
ours is by the existence of so many monied corporations. They are giant powers, and a constant menace
to freedom, dangerous in proportion to their wealth.

The public interest demands that Banking, Insurance, and Railroad corporations, land monopoly, and
manufacturing monopolies be suppressed, and the
government assume control of these interests, and that
the kinds of property that money shall represent and
be exchangable for, be particularly defined, limited and
circumscribed by legislative enactments. Then money becomes a harmless acquisition. Then might eve-
ery man have and hold all the money he may. The

public has reason to complain of the laws giving to the monied class dangerous monopolies, and especially the monopoly of furnishing exchange to the country. The fountain from which all exchange should flow and directly to the people, is the government. Then if interest be paid the State for the use of money, it becomes a government tax, lessening the tax on other property, and benefitting everybody—instead of building up a hateful, privileged class of respectable paupers, living without labor, through usury—a monopoly inherited from the parent Britain, along with slavery, and that must, like slavery, be got rid of— and speedily—for it is fast hurrying the nation into bankdruptey.

Think not that America is destined to follow the footsteps of Europe. She will make a path for herself. This new world was prepared by Providence as the garden of the Lord in which new and better ideas are to germinate and grow, and be carried from this new land and transplanted in the old. What produced the French Revolution in the days of Washington? American ideas. I do not say that our best ideas of government are native of this soil. I know whence our freedom has arisen. I know who is the author of our liberty. That one germ idea—equality of men—is traced rightfully back to the Friend of the Poor—the denouncer of the rich, but His thought could not work in the old world as in the new, the leven of gentleness and love being there neutralized by antagonistic institutions—arbitrary governments and corporations —kings, lords and designing priests. Old world customs and institutions take root here and grow for a time and then wither. The climate is not suited to them. The new world has never known anything but freedom. The old world customs belong to depotism. The new world will beget its own governments, customs, institutions; but top off all will be freedom. There is no doubt of this. Private and corporate wealth may array itself against liberty—then private and corporate wealth must go to the wall, until the commonwealth only shall survive. Thus will equality be realized the subordination of riches to the general good, the suppression of class distinctions. I look for the time to come in America when no man will build a costlier house than his neighbor, the grand works of art and architecture will be public, like the Pantheon. There will then be uniformity of hours of labor and recrea-

tion, general comfort, but no private wealth, the
same advantages being open to all, schools free, the-
atrical entertainments free (as in acient Athens), lectures free, librairies free. There will be no "legal"
methods of getting suddenly rich, then; for all such
methods, though tolerated now, as human slavery
was a few years ago, are, like human slavery, wrong—
yea, wicked. Do you not see that it is wrong for me
to seize upon and appropriate to my own use the proceeds of others' labor, gathering around me a mountain of the surplus products of industry, stpping to
destitution the producers of those products, whether
I do this by the use of the *slave whip*, or by any other
means? My own weak arm can produce little.
Why must others serve me, toil and sweat for me,
pour out the fruits of their toil at *my* feet until I
have become a millionaire? What magnetic power
is there in my physical structure to attract to me all
this surplus wealth, as the water flows to the sea? I
am only a man, nor has God made me in any respect
dissimilar to other men. It is the unjust laws that
favor me. God gave me my *manhood*. The laws of
my country regard not God-given manhood; they
favor only *wealth*. The laws cause wealth to attract
to itself wealth by giving the wealthy certain *monopolies*. Wealth being the product of labor and mechanical skill, is of slow growth naturally. It comes
not suddenly to the world. The ratio of annual increase of wealth in the United States is little more
than three per cent; $7,000,000,000 the average annual
product, divided by 45,000,000 inhabitants gives $155
per capita——or $1,000 for each adult male citizen. So,
do you not see that there is no such thing as justly
acquiring sudden wealth. The John Jacob Astors of
the world have got their great wealth mainly by
"robbing widows' houses."

This contest for the rights of man will continue
until the cause of the people completely triumph. It
is the same struggle as of 1776, between our fathers
and the king and the lords of England, and as of 1640
in England between the Roundhead and the Caval-
ier—the friction of advancing civilization, the idea
of equality going forward to its realization. We
may truly say the same to-day that McCauley said in
the British parliament years ago: "At this very
moment," he said, "we everywhere see society outgrow
ing our institutions. * * * Here we see the bar-

barism of the 13th century coupled with the civilization of the 19th, and we see, too, that this barbarism belongs to the government and the civilization to the people. Then, I say, that this incongruous state of things cannot continue, and if we do not terminate it with wisdom ere long, we shall find it ended with violence."

The barbarism that environs us is the institutions brought over from England that are still cumbering the ground here, banking institutions, insurance institutions, individual capital employing labor extensively, land monopoly, and all sorts of private monied corporations, organized and conducted on selfish principles, and building up the power and wealth of the few at the expense of the many. Those who have power in their hands, as all history shows, never give it up voluntarily. It must be wrenched from them. And the monopolies which the ages have handed down through the centuries of the tyrannous, monarchial, aristocratic past, and that are now held by the few to the detriment of the many, must be put down by the same power that has overcome monarchy; suppressed aristocracy; blotted out African slavery and lifted up the laboring classes here, *the power of the popular will.* Concentrated capital and monopolies will soon become so burdensome that they must be thrown down by universal consent. A few giant firms ere long will transact all the business, and tens of thousands of buildings heretofore occupied by small shop-keepers, grocers, merchants, etc. will stand vacant. The lands will soon be monopolized by a few here as in Europe—all manufacturing will be done by a few great capitalists; the pork-packing of the northwest by two or three gigantic firms of Chicago, St. Louis and Cincinnati, under the control of European capitalists, as the carrying trade of the whole nation is now principally under the control of three great, swollen barnacles—Gould, Scott and Vanderbilt. Thus will all business be controlled by a syndicate of money kings, with headquarters in London, and become such a monopoly that producers and consumers cannot endure it, and they will find relief in co-operative stores, co-operative factories, etc., and the people of America will be forced, of necessity, to take governmental control of all transportation interests, as of the mails, and goods be forwarded, like letters stamped, so much per pound or cwt. The people, acting individually, cannot compete with monopolies. Monopolies will conquer the masses in detail unless the masses concentrate their power and enforce their will through the laws. We have about come upon a period in the world's history when there is no alternative left us but the inauguration of an absolute control by the people, through legislation, of all interests—a complete crystalization of the popular will in perfected institutions. "Associations" of all kinds are combined now against the masses, and arbitrarily levy tax for support, more absolute in their tyranny than was Charles I. even. The masses must combine in a gigantic union with articles of association which shall be the fundamental constitutions of State and National governments, instituted for the common welfare alone.

Labor, indeed, is master of the situation. The toilers are the ninety and nine. They make and run all the machinery—build and operate all the railroads.. They build all forts, and man them ; they manufacture all guns and implements of war, and use them ! Whose muscular arms load and fire the cannons ? Whose sinewy hands grasp the swords and muskets ? Of what class of society was that grand army of Grant and Sherman composed that passed in review before President Johnson at Washington in 1865 ? and of Lee and Johnson that was disbanded and sent home ? Toilers, and toilers alone ! They are the all in all. They are the lords and gods of this great world. Whenever the people are ready the great change will come. There will be no war ; for there will be nobody to fight against combined labor. You cannot set even the laboring men of England to fight against the laboring men of the United States. The *people* will go to war no more. The only way possible for capital to conquer labor (and that is no longer possible) were to set the laborers fighting one another, as the whites have the Indians ever. Thus the toilers of the north and the toilers of the south were forced by party leaders in 1861 into a war that the people would never have gone into of their own voice and choice. Wars will cease when the people rule. The people have never ruled yet; but they soon will. A solid South and a solid North can never be set shooting each other again. Labor will take care of itself. Capitalists would now shape the results of the war of '61, so that instead of having been, as we supposed, the triumph of free labor over slave labor, it would prove to have been the triumph of Wall street and Lombard street capialists over the agriculturalists, manufacturers and laborers of North America. Instead of emancipating labor, and giving freedom to four millions of slaves, it would prove to have enslaved forty millions of freemen, unless the present policy of gold resumption be given up. But this will end. The reaction will come---and in spite of a venal and corrupt press---and the gigantic power of monied monopolies and corporations the people will rule. Labor will soon be master. What is unbearable will not be borne---and the evils that are now upon us are unbearable. *A national convention to revise the federal constitution will soon be demanded. It will assemble; and it will never adjourn until the government is brought into harmony with the changed condition of things, and the flag made the emblem of freedom and equality.*

When this is accomplished, instead of the laws being made in the interest of selfishness, they will enforce the golden rule ; and when this is done, the Kingdom of God is established on the earth. This is all that I pray for ; this is all I contend for : this is what I would *die* for. It is the establishment of such a community of love that the angels foresaw when they proclaimed peace on earth good will towards men. This is the Apocalyptic New Jerusalem that was revealed to the banished saint on the Isle of Patmos "descending from God out of heaven ;" the "new earth" when the "first earth had passed away" and "God should dwell with men and be their God and they should be His people." This glorious Kingdom of God is rapidly descending upon our earth---1976 will behold it. The grand progress of mind during the last century is the harbinger of the coming day. Man has nearly ceased to be a savage. He is almost ripe---and beautiful will be the cluster upon the vine of love.

Ralph Waldo Emerson says : "The idea which now begins to agitate society, has a wider scope than our daily employments---our households and the institutions of property. We are to revise the whole of our social structure---the state, the school, religion, marriage, trade, science, and explore the foundation of our nature. What is man born for but to be a reformer---a *re-maker* of what man has made—a renouncer of lies -a restorer of truth and good, imitating the great nature which embosoms us all, and which sleeps no moment on an old *past;* but every hour repairs herself, yielding us every morning a new day, and with every pulsation a new life. Let him remove everything which is not true to him.   *   *   There will dawn ere long on our p litics, on our modes of living, a nobler morning in the sentiment of love. Our age and history of these thousand years has not been the history of kindness ; but of selfishness. Our distrust is very expensive. The money spent for courts and prisons is ill-laid out. We make by distrust the thief, the burglar, and incendiary, and by our court and jail we keep him so. An acceptance of the sentiment of love throughout Christendom for a season, would bring the felon and outcast to our side in tears. with the devotion of his faculties to our service. See this wide society of laboring men and women. We allow ourselves to be served by them ; we live apart from them and meet them on the street without a salute. We do not greet their talents, nor rejoice in their good fortune, nor foster their hopes, nor in the assembly of the people vote fer what is dear to them Thus we enact the part of the selfish noble and king to the world's foundation.   *   *

    *   Let our affections flow out to our fellows ; it would operate in a day the greatest of all revolutlons. THE STATE MUST CONSIDER THE POOR NAN AND ALL VOICES MUST SPEAK FOR HIM. EVERY CHILD BORN MUST HAVE A JUST CHANCE (WITH WORK) FOR HIS BREAD.''

And James Freeman Clarke says : "The time will come at last--long foretold by prophet and sybil, long retarded by unbelief and formalism---when wars shall cease, and the reign of just laws take the place of force in the great federation of mankind.   *   * Christ will at last become in reality the Prince of *Peace*, putting and end to war between nations, war between classes in society, war between criminals and the state. In trade, instead of competition. we shall have co-operation, and all industry will receive its just recompence."

PART III.—THE RIGHTS OF LABOR.

(TAKEN FROM A BOOK OF THE AUTHOR'S OF THE ABOVE TITLE PRINTED IN 1875.)

What progress the grand principles of the NEW PARTY, that as yet has won no conquests, but is one day to rule America and the world, have made among the thinking men of our age and country ! That party is the Party of Labor—and the impending conflict is between labor and capital.

There is nothing more plainly discernable than the coming revolution in favor of the rights of the laboring man, or, I should say, the rights of man : for the rights of labor and the rights of man are identical. By and through labor come subsistence and all wealth—or as President Grant expresses it in his message of December, 1874, "the working man must, after all, produce the wealth." No man is exempt from the natural obligation to earn his living by the sweat of his face. It is true many men do live by the sweat of other men's faces, but this is not as it should be. All able-bodied men should earn their own living by their own labor ; and every artificial advantage given to one man over another by the unjust laws, should be removed, and all men left exactly upon the same plane of equality. This must come about as soon as despotic government is broken up, and the people universally govern. The rights of individuals cannot be protected until the world has freed itself from the domination of wealth.

The struggle of the common people for their inalienable rights is not the battle of a day, but of centuries. It goes on with the progress of enlightenment. The victory will be won when the divinity of humanity has been completely recognized in the universal thought of men. The foolish homage so long given to wealth will then be replaced by homage to manhood.

"A man's a man for a' that,"

is the germ-idea of civilization—the corner stone of the temple of freedom.

The most powerful agents are the most subtile. · Ideas ar· irresistible. When our fathers announced " We hold these truths to be self-evident that all men are created equal; and are endowed by their Creator with the inalienable rights of life, liberty, and the pursuit of happiness," the irrepressible conflict between freedom and slavery began in the new world. The poor black man was held under no worse servitude than the poor white is held to-day.

The poor man has ever been a slave to the rich. Great the friction this onward moving idea was destined to encounter. Blood must flow like water ; but the idea must move on and on ; and just so sure as the world is destined to emerge from darkness into light, from barbarism into civilization, *equality must come.*

"Still it moves"—the pondrous world still rolls upon its axis, and the truths of God advance. The mills of ths gods are slowly grinding out the inevitable. In the atmosphere of America--clear as the mountain atmosphere of Colorado—the bright dome of the temple of freedom stands out against the horizon as if but a little way off. But before the people shall enter that temple *"equal"* dreadful conflicts must even yet be had. The hosts of slavery must be further overcome—they must be routed and driven from the very " last ditch." Not an inch of ground will the enemy yield except it be taken from him by mighty force.

When announced "all are created equal," our people were, for more than a hundred years, destined to wander in the wilderness ere this ideal could be replaced by the real. The war of Revolution snuffed out the "king" idea, and that of a "titled nobility." Slowly and surely have the people been advancing. The public conscience could no longer tolerate the flaunting lie of chattel slavery written upon our escutcheon. That devil "went out hard," but it had to go, because our fathers had declared for human equality.

But another step forward will soon be taken by the American nation—another step towards the full realization of the idea of the Declaration of Independence. The storm-cloud is gathering. One even now may behold it, "larger than a man's hand." Millions of earnest men and women in this United States, North and South, are united as one in the determination tha·

the poor man shall have his rights- that intelligence
and numbers; and not "capital" shall rule the nation.

"Chattel slavery," they assert, "has been abolished ;
but the rights and relations of labor stand just where
they did before the emancipation, in respect to the di-
visions of its products. The difference lies only in
the methods of abstracting the results and concentra-
them in the hands of a few capitalists. Capital is now
the master and dictates the terms, and thus all labor
ers are practically placed in the same condition as the
slave before the emancipation,"

Strong language indeed, and big with meaning.
Thus spoke the farmers and workingmen of Indiana
in State Convention, assembled at Indianapolis, on
the 10th day of June, 1874 :

"We need only point," they say, "to the fact that in
this benificent country of unlimited resources, with
the land annually groaning beneath the products of
human effort, the mass of the people have no supply
beyond their daily wants, and are compelled, from unjust conditions, in sickness or misfortune, to become
paupers. Pauperism and crime are the perplexing
questions of all modern statesmanship, and it is with
these we have to deal. How far these evils are con-
nected with the abuses inflicted on labor, a superficial
statesmanship seems not to perceive."

They point out as the instrumentality by which
these wrongs are inflicted :

"First—Banking and monied monopolies, by which,
through ruinous rates of interest, the products of hu:
man labor are concentrated into the hands of non-
producers. This is the great central source of these
wrongs, in and through which all other monopolies
exist and operate.

"Second—Consolidated railroads and other transit
monopolies, whereby all industries are taxed to the
last mill they will bear for the benefit of the stock-
holders and stock-jobbers.

"Third—Manufacturing monopolies, whereby all
small operators are crushed out and the prices of labor and products are determined with mathematical
certainty in the interest of the capitalists.

"Fourth—Land monopolies, by which the public domain is absorbed by a few corporations and speculators.

"Fifth—Commercial and grain monopolies, and
speculation enriching the bloated corporations on human necessities."·

The working men and farmers then announce it to
be their aim to "restore the government to its original
purpose," which they define to be to "protect property
and enforce natural rights." "We desire," they say,
"a proper equality and protection for the weak, and
restraint upon the strong : in short, justly distributed
burdens and justly distributed powers." These, they
affirm are American ideas, the very essence of American independence, and to "advocate the contrary is
unworthy the sons and daughters of an American
Republic."

Who is so blind that he does not "discern the signs
of the times ?" There is near at hand a struggle that
will "try men's souls." If you, reader, have in you
the heart of a patriot, it will be warmed with emo-
tions of love for your country, and like a true man,
you will be found in the ranks of the common people,
contending for the immortal principle of human
equality. If you are contaminated with venality—if
you have in you the heart of a Benedict Arnold—the
rich capitalist will enlist you on his side, for he has
in his possession the money bag ; and by bribery, by
the aid of a venal press, and base appeals to the basest
passions of the base, he will endeavor to rally to his
standard his hireling supporters, and by their aid
strive to keep down under his feet the working population of this nation.

Years ago, when I read of the efforts of the laboring men of Europe for their rights, as shown in the
aims and objects of the International Society, I said,
"when the working men and farmers of America begin in earnest to strike for their rights, then will my
heart be enlisted in the great cause, and so long as the
Good Being shall see fit to preserve my life, will I battle with tongue and pen to hasten on the period when
the glorious dream of Jefferson shall be realized, and
all be indeed equal." I believe the time is not far distant in the history of this country, when the laws
shall be so perfect and the administration of them so
complete, that there will be practical equality among
the people and the divine command "thou shalt love
thy fellow man as thyself," be practically enforced as
the supreme law of the land.

That "all men are created equal," implies that practical equality ought to be maintained among men,
else it is a meaningless expression, so far as the rights

4*

of men are concerned.   It means that in society all
are by nature equal, and no artificial fetters ought to
be permitted to bind the hands of any.   The track
should be clear, so that all might have an even chance
in the race toward the goal of mental and moral per-
fection.   There should be no hindrances set up by the
laws or customs, or conditions of society, to any ; but
every child born ought to have an ev n start with every other child,   Inequality of conditions exists among
men because governments and laws are immature.
The few should not be permitted to clutch the surplus
wealth of the nation ; but all surplus wealth should
be in the possession of the State, for the common benefit, that the youth of the land may be completely educated and protected from pauperism and prepared
for the sublime office of citizenship.

We may define a true and perfect government or
commonwealth, in the words of the divine teacher of
men, "Thou shalt love thy fellow man as thyself."
The object of good government is to compel the performance of the natural obligations of man to man.
It is true that government cannot directly *compel* man
to *love* his fellow man ; but it is the office of the
school master to instil into the minds of youth the
sentiments of love and patriotism, and fidelity and
duty. Government is responsible for the education
of the people.   To the government we must look to
encourage and support those schools and institutions
of learning that shall lead all citizens to realize their
obligations to each other and to society.   Government
should enforce the duties resulting from the natural
obligation to love our fellow man as ourself.   Our
free school sytem is based on this fact.   Many individuals pay taxes to educate the children of poor men
who would not give a cent for that purpose voluntarily.   The government compels the performance of
this grand duty.   The government should crystalize
in its laws the command, "Love thy neighbor as thyself."

Let us see for a moment what kind of society or
state that would be in which this divine law was practically carried out and enforced.   No fraternity could
be bound more closely in its obligations of charity.
Every child would be bountifully clothed, fed and
completely educated, cared for and protected.   Every
widow and every orphan would receive a bountiful
pension.   Who would fail to love such a government ?

Who would not be willing to die in defence of such
noble institutions? There would be no such word
known as "selfishness" in such a well ordered society.
Every one would live and labor for other's good and
not for his own. He would be *compelled* to do so,
whether he felt like doing so or not, as every rich
man is compelled to pay taxes to support free schools,
though some sordid ones bite their lips with indignation because compelled to contribute to the education
of others' children. But the law says to him, " Thou
shalt love thy neighbor as thyself." "thou *shalt* love,"
so far as to give willingly or unwillingly of thy substance for the education of the children of thy unfortunate or less prosperous neighbor. His children thou
must bless—with thy money paid into the public school
fund —willingly or unwillingly, thou shalt, so far as
thy actions are concerned, practically "love thy neighbor as thyself." But our free school system is only
the shadow of good things to come. The pensions
given to orphans and widows of soldiers who fell in
the service, are but the shadow of good things to come.
Every widow and every orphan will one day, in this
free and happy Republic, draw pension from government—not as paupers—but as rightful heirs ; for each
good and true citizen will say, "Every mother in
America is my mother." I will assume to be the father of the fatherless. I will do all in my power to
have it said, "it is good for a child to be born." If it
is right that we should love our fellow men as ourself, the State is obligated to enforce the practical ob-
servance of all actions properly growing out of this
duty. Every person living under the shadow of this
divine law has rights growing out of this law. It is
the duty of the government to enforce natural rights.
It is a natural law shat the father shall love his children. His duty is to watch over and protect his child.
The law of the land punishes the parent for neglect;
for there is such a thing as "criminal neglect." The
father must fulfill the duties and obligations of a
father. The child can demand protection. The child
has rights growing out of its condition as a helpless,
dependent child. The law of the land must enforce
the natural obligation of the father to protect his
child. If it is the supreme law of God and nature
that we should love our fellow man as ourself, then it
is the office of government to *enforce the obligation
growing out of this divine law.* Love is, and has

52   APPENDIX.

ever been held by the enlightened, the supreme law. It was engraven on a tomb of one of the Pharaos at Thebes, more than three thousand years ago, "I have given bread to the hungry; water to the thirsty; clothes to the naked, and shelter to the stranger." Four thousand years look down upon the saying of the Rig Veda, "The kind mortal is greater than the greatest in heaven."

To this law of love all laws must ultimately be conformed. Whatever is contray to love must one day come to an end. "I know," says Theodore Parker, "man will triumph over matter; the people over tyrants; right over wrong; truth over falsehood; love over hate." Upon the ultimate, final and complete triumph of love hangs the hope of the universe. The world becomes civilized as men learn to love one another. Stop the onward progress of a divine idea, who can! Selfishness and cruelty must perish. What a change will come over the face of this world! Armies will one day cease to muster for war. Navies will ride the seas no more. Complete equality will prevail among men. The freedom and happiness of every individual will be secure. Each will practically love his neighbor as himself. I repeat, inequality of conditions exists among men because governments and laws are immature. Man is yet a savage. Oh, if we could but lift the curtain of the future and behold the glorious panorama of the world as it will be when the people have got full control of all States, and when kings and priests and aristocrats shall be unknown, then would we behold a picture that would gladden every heart. The ponderous roller of enlightened reason, truth and love, must yet pass over the world, leveling all inequalities of condition. The time will come when mankind will indeed be one family, and when one child of God will be just as well off as another. Is God the father of us all, and are we all brethren and joint inheritors of this world, when a few get all and the many nothing? Yes, every child born ought to have an even start with every other child. Is not this God's world, and are not all alike his offspring? Why then should the few be permitted to clutch the surplus wealth of the nations?

It is worth while to note particularly how inequalty of conditions among men is brought about. Money gained by honest industry is bestowed by God.

By industry, it is said we gain wealth ; but this saying is false, No man can by honest industry become
very wealthy. It is not by industry great fortunes
have been gained. Look at the great landed estates
possessed by the feudal lords of Europe. In the middle ages all Europe was subjugated by the Gothic and
Vandal tribes. The chiefs divided up the lands between themselves, and (as in England,) the law of
primogeniture has brought down the landed estates
whole and unbroken to the descendants of those military chiefs.

Any one can see that these chiefs looked only to
their own selfish interests and of their posterity. The
laws were made in the interest of the rich. The sons
of the lords are all provided for by the laws of England, even to-day. The church and the army furnish
"sinecures," "livings," large "pay,"to the sons of the
rich only. Thus it has ever been that selfishness has
cursed the world ; for nearly all the laws that govern
mankind to-day have been dictated by selfishness.
The inalienable rights of man have not been regar-
ded, but only the interests of the ruling class—the
rich.

We are accustomed to consider that to be right which
is legitimate, which is lawful. Is it right for a very few
men to own the lands of England, Ireland and Scotland? Those few are a privileged class. They do no
manual labor, but they are supported by the toil and
sweat of other men, whom God designed to be their
equals, and who are their peers in all respects but that
these monopolize the earth that God has designed to
be as free as the air we breathe and the water we
drink. They hold this land by the same right
that the slave-master of the south held his
slave—by the law of force—and not by any
natural right. It is amazing that in this enlightend
age, when in all lands, it is conceded by all fair-mind-
ed men, that all just government is founded on the
sovereignty and cousent of the governed, and that its
purpose is to protect the weak and restrain the strong
—enforcing natural rights—it is amazing I say, that
the oppressed millions of England, Ireland and Scotland do not assert their rights to the equal protection
of the laws, and bring down the land monopolists to
the same level as other men—dividing up the lands
equitably among the people to whom it rightfully belongs. How much better are those landlords than

were the slave-buyers and slave-sellers of the South? They seize upon and appropriate to their own use the profits of other men's labor.

The first thing in importance to the happiness of mankind is the suppression of monopoly in lands. God and nature give no right to any man of any more of earth's surface than when tilled by his own hands will supply his necessities. The only right that any man can set up to any more than an equitable portion of God's domain is the "legal" right. The common law favoring land monopoly has come down to us from the dark ages, when might made right, and when a few military cheiftains divided habitable Europe between themselves. holding the rest of mankind as vassals and serfs. The common law founded in wrong ought not to be considered binding to-day. The statute laws of the country are made by the people, and the people will not always be willing to let the few alone reap advantage from the laws. Individual rights does not mean the privilege of the individual to plunder his neighbors. No man has a right to grasp more than his just share of God's gifts to His children. The same arguments must be resorted to, to justify land monopoly as were used to justify human slavery. When the few own all the lands the people are not better off than were the negro slaves of the South. Land monopoly places the many under the heels of the few, destroying the independence and happiness of the great majority of mankind, reducing them to practical vassalage. When the few own all the lands, they dictate to the many the terms on which they will allow them to live at all. In this country land rents are becoming higher and higher. In England and Ireland the tiller of the soil gets only a tithe of the profits of his own labor while the landlord seizes upon the bulk. The laborer is reduced to the greatest indigence, while the land-lord wallows in luxury. The time will come in this country when the landless will be in the condition of the Irish peasantry, unless there comes the change that I anticipate.

Let it be a fundamental law that no man can hold lands that he does not occupy, and that his homestead shall be a limited number of acres (say 40, 80, or 160) of tillable land. Let the surplus lands be appraised, and the owners paid for them by the State, and let the State then sell the lands to the landless on equitable terms until every acre shall be cultivated by the actual owners.

That a half dozen men do not own every acre of land in Iowa, is not that there is not that many men in the United States able to purchase every acre nor that there is any law to prevent; but that they can make more out of their money at present by lending it at ten per cent to individuals at the same time that government pays them from five to seven per cent on the same in gold. But the testimony comes up from the Atlantic States and the Middle States, that the land is gravitating into a few hands. Every patriot should feel alarmed at the prospect of America's becoming like England and Ireland a land in which the laborer is held down under a servile yoke. As soon as the country becomes settled, and there are no more wild lands, then will the fetters begin to press down into the flesh of the tiller of the soil. The capitalist will be king, and the reign of Caligula will be mild compared to the rule of the land monopolists. Already the people can scarcely bear up under the yoke—but at present it is as "soft as downy pillows are," compared to what 't will be. See what miserable pig-stys are erected for the renter to live in on the large farms to-day ; at the same time that the land owner dwells in a fine mansion, and stables his horses in a building that costs ten dollars to where the renter's cabin costs ten cents. And how will it be when there are no more homesteads to be taken ? And what will the tiller of the soil receive when he finds himself "bound hand and foot," and at the mercy of his landlord ? He will be a poor, miserable, beggar slave! worse off than was the negro slave of the South, for the master will not be bound to support him in sickness and old age, as was the slave master bound to support his negro slaves while they lived. Land monopoly and the slave system belong together. They are twin relics of barbarism. The slave system of the southern Confederacy was a merciful system compared to that of a few owning all the lands, and being free from the obligation to feed, clothe and watch over their farm laborers all their lives,

The elements, air, water and land belong to man by an inalienable right. You might as well monopolize air and water as land. You might as well buy and sell men as to monopolize the land. You violate a natural right the same in the one case as in the other. I have a right to life. I cannot live without land. I have a natural right to liberty. I cannot be free without land. I have a natural right to the pursuit of happiness. I cannot maintain this right without land. Why argue this question, when we have Ireland before us, and Scotland, yea, and even good old England?

The land monopolist holds his acres by the law of force, just as the slave-master held his slave. He has no right to any more land than is necessary to his support. He has a right to a patch six feet long and three feet wide when he is dead, for a grave, (unless happily cremation steps in,) and while he lives he has a natural right to just so much land as when tilled by his own hands will supply his necessities, and no more—and "possession is ownership." It is not his when he has abandoned it. The land by right belongs to the man that plows it, as the air belongs to the man that breathes it, and the water to the man that drinks it. There is land enough in the United States alone, suitable for tillage, to give every man in the world that lives by tilling the soil, forty acres. Why then need any American be poor and want for bread?

Eight miles north-west from the city of Des Moines is almost an entire township of land, with scarcely a house on it—virgin prairie land, beautiful and rich, as is to be found in the world; the sod as yet unbroken by the plow, while the land all around is in cultivation. Here might be dwelling hundreds (I might almost say thousands) of happy families; but a few speculators in Boston and New York are holding it for a big price. What grants of public domain have been given to railroad companies! When the government will allow one man to own thousands of acres of land and thus retard its settlement, or give him control over the liberty of his fellows, it is a monstrous abuse; but when it grants millions of acres to corporations, language fails—words cannot express the magnitude of the wrong.

A just government will protect property and enforce natural rights. It will not protect property in man but it will enforce the natural right of every man to life, liberty and the pursuit of happiness. It will not protect the individual in the unjust privilege of owning more land than is needful for his support; but it will enforce the natural right of every man to land

enough to afford him subsistence. Every man has a
natural right to the field that he tills.

"The earth is the Lord's and the fullness thereof."
God has bestowed this bountiful gift upon the children
of men; nor did he say "a few may monopolize the
land;" but the voice of Truth, which is the voice of
God, declares "all men are created equal," all have
by nature the same right to this earth and its fullness.
The laws of States and nations cannot abrogate the
laws of God.

Two boys attend the same school! They are of
equal age, of equal strength, of equal health, recite
in the same classes, are of equal intelligence. They
graduate at the same time, both having the same
standing in their classes. They go into business. The
one uses as much industry as the other, and is as dili-
gent in business, exercising as much thought and intelligence, and physical power. The one makes perhaps five hundred dollars per day; the other not more
than five dollars per day. Why the difference? The
question is answered in one word—CAPITAL. The one
is rich and has capital to invest. The other is poor
and depends upon industry alone. This is all legitimate. but is it right? What equality is there here?
It is legal but not right. The laws are framed to help
the rich. From the feudal ages down to the present
time, wealth has in reality dictated all the laws. They
bear hard upon labor. Money increases by its own
growth, so to speak. To be sure gold buried in the
ground will not increase; but by the laws and customs of society, the possessor of money may double
his fortune every ten years. In the language of Des
Moines' greatest banker and capitalist,* "Ten per cent
interest will eat the world up." This is a great wrong;
for thus the few gather the increasing wealth of the
State. I lay this down as a fundamental truth; THE
LAW THAT ALLOWS ONE MAN TO RECEIVE MORE THAN
ANOTHER FOR THE SAME AMOUNT OF PHYSICAL OR
MENTAL TOIL, IS WRONG. The times are out of joint
when one man can gather a thousand dollars as the
fruit of one day's labor while another man working
just as hard cannot make five dollars to save his life..

All wealth comes primarily from the ground, and is
brought forth by the plow. What large cities are to
be seen on the deserts? What habitations of men?
But go where the soil is rich and productive and you

*B. F. Allen

behold population and cities. Where men have to devote every moment of their time to the procuring of their daily bread, there can be no accumulation of wealth. Where bread fails nothing else has any value. In the heart of the Sahara desert Crœsus starving might vainly cry "A million of dollars for a loaf of bread." If the world were all barren, so that men could barely, by constant labor, procure food and clothing, there could be no accumulation of capital. Gold could have no value where there was nothing to exchange it for, though one possessed as much as is in the vaults of the bank of England. Money represents surplus products. If there were no products of labor beyond what would satisfy the immediate wants of the producers. money could have no value whatever. Food is first to be looked after, and the abundance or scarcity of food regulates the price of all other products ; for one might be in condition to sell even his birthright for a mess of pottage.

It takes nearly all the farmer's surplus grain to pay his taxes. Unless he is to some extent a capitalist, unless he can seize upon the profits of other men's labor, either by holding them as slaves and working them on his plantations, as was the case in the South, or else by robbing them of their hard earnings after the manner of the English landlord, the farmer cannot become rich ; because the soil has a limit to its productiveness, and there is a limit to the amount of work one man can do. No vote of House or Senate can make mother earth yield the farmer fifty thousand dollars per year salary, which is equivalent to fifty thousand bushels of wheat. The average yield of wheat per acre is fifteen bushels. It would require ne man to plow sow and reap 3333$\frac{1}{3}$ acreas of wheat to yield fifty thousand dollar's worth at the rate of one dollar per bushel. God pays the farmer his salary and it is not a large salary either. One man can farm with his own individual labor not more than eighty acres of tillable land, even of our beautiful prairie, and with the aid of all modern machinery and improved farm implements into the bargain. This might produce in wheat an average per year of twelve hundred bushels, or, in corn, twenty-four hundred bushels. So, about *twelve hundred dollars per year is all God pays the farmer for his toil.* "By the sweat of thy face thou shalt eat bread." Out of this the farmer has to pay for farm implements and machinery,

taxes for the support of Government, purchase clothing and shoes for his family, groceries, etc. The per
diem of the farmer is less than five bushels of wheat
or ten bushels of corn. The point that I would make
is this: If any human being grasps the price of one
hundred bushels of wheat for his days labor, he vir-
tually steals ninety-five bushels of wheat. If he
seizes upon only the price of one hundred bushels of
corn for his days' work he steals only ninety bushels
of corn. Whoever on the face of this earth, where
all men are by nature equal, grasps more as the price
of his days labor than God pays the industrious farmer, is a theif and a robber to that extent, and this is
one great cause of the inequality of conditions among
men.

Since the farmer is limited by the fiat of God, in the
amount of his daily earnings, all men should be limited to like extent, by the laws and customs of the
country. One mans wages should be just the same
as another's, and no more.

But the rich capitalist is allowed by the laws to
skim all the cream off the hard earnings of the toiling millions. Thus the laws allow a portion of mankind to seize upon what rightfully belongs to another
portion ; thus anarchy reigns, and the rights of property are not enforced, guarded or protected.

Does not every man serve his country that has an
honorable occupation ? Are not all public servants
that labor ? I say that every industrious citizen is as
much a servant of the public as is the president of the
United States. The farmer serves the state by producing what renders the state habitable. He is a
more important official than presidents or kings. Let
the conditions of society be such that every man
must follow so ne useful occupation, and let no employment bring higher compensation than the industrious farmer receives from the hand of God. Let an
equitable price for daily labor be established, based
upon the bounty of mother earth. When no man
can monopolize more than his just share of earth's
products, (all who are alike industrious receiving like
pay,) then all may have ample leisure for mental
culture and social enjoyment ; but under the present
unjust and barbarous system, the many are robbed of
almost all privilege of culture and enjoyment.

Society should be so crystalized that every man
would occupy an important place in it and feel his

responsibility to the public as if elected to the office. It is one man's office to raise grain; another's to make shoes for the public ; another's to work in iron ; another's to work in wood, etc.; all are officials doing service for the State, and should be so recognized, and their salaries made sure ; and when they become old and worn out in the public service, they deserve to draw a pension as much as any retired army officer.

That all are public officials who can deny? Can the state be maintained, and leave off agriculture and the mechanical arts? Are not the men devoted to these pursuits, essential elements of the commonwealth? Yea, *the* essential elements. Are they not as important as soldiers to an army? And if the State makes provision for her soldiers why not for her citizens devoted to her service, as are the farmers and mechanics? Should not the State see, at least that these upbuilders of all civilization are protected in their rights, and not plundered and robbed of their rightful earnings? It should watch over them like a parent from the cradle to the grave.

But some, it is said, have spent much time and money to gain good education, and ought they not receive higher wages for their labor than those who have no education? President Grant has prepared himself for his high office by much study and [sacrifice: ought he not receive higher wages than the common farmer that feeds a threshing machine? The thresher needs little knowledge of books, say you, to fit him for his office, and why should he expect as much for his time and labor as General Grant?

I would try to answer this by saying that according to our theory of government, the State owes every child a good education. The state is expected to prepare its citizens for the office of citizenship : hence our free schools, universities, agricultural colleges, etc., supported at the public charge. General Grant was educated by the government for the profession of the soldier : another boy is prepared by the State in its schools and colleges for the office of the farmer. The State should not be partial, but treat all its children alike. If the State has been partial to General Grant, and has given him better opportunities of acquiring knowledge than it gave the poor farmer that feeds the threshing machine, must the latter be punished all his life for the State's neglect? Must his family be punished and starved for the State's

having made a pet of one of its children, and neg-
lected another?

One man's children deserve education as well as
another's, and one man is suppposed to have as great
burdens to bear as another. It is the allotted portion of each man to bring up his family. No man
can have any greater work than this to do, unless he
has the privilege of nursing his aged parents, or of
supporting his orphaned brothers and sisters ; but as
a rule one man's needs are reckoned as great as the
needs of another, and therefore one man's income
should be equal to that of another.

The primary object of all human effort is subsis
tence. It is to be presumed that it requires as much
to subsist one as another, therefore the income of each
should be the same.

There is a great struggle going on in this country,
no less mighty and important because silent and with
out force of arms. The mouse that ate the cable off,
worked silently, but diligently, and the consequence
was, that wanting the cable, the ship was lost. Capital is gnawing off the cable—aye, it is perforating
the bottom of the great Ship of State, as if a million
of worms were boring gimlet holes through it, until
soon the floods will come pouring in and the ship go
to the bottom of the sea and there remain for ever
unless the people awaken from their slumber of false
security and betake themselves to work at the pumps
for dear life.

The people begin to see the danger that lies in excessive wealth in the hands of individuals and petty
corporations. It appears to be the rule that as a man
increases his wealth, he loses his patriotism, and
when he becomes a millionaire, he scruples not to enter the halls of legislation, to turn by bribery, if possible the representatives of the people from the path
of duty. His vanity leads him to suppose that by his
superior wisdom he has gotten all his great fortune,
and that every man that is poor, is so because he is a
practical fool, and that, therefore, republican government is, after all a farce. "Let the poor man be disfranchised" will be the demand made by the rich man
after a while. Rob the people of all their substance
first, and then take from them their only means of
protection against actual enslavement—the ballot.
Pampered politicians will be found ready to betray
the people, and to connive at the disfranchisement

of the toilers, in the cities, first and afterward in the State at large on the plea that "only tax payers ought to vote."

The people have about come to the conclusion that if rich men and bloated corporations are the natural enemies to freedom and free government, great wealth shall not longer be allowed to concentrate in the hands of individuals and petty corporations, but must be poured into the lap of the State alone. If capital in the hands of individuals and petty corporations is in actual antagonism to human freedom and equality, we must suppress the enemy at all hazards. No man must be permitted to accumulate a vast fortune if the danger lies here. The government of the people, by the people, for the people must be maintained.

Who is to blame if a revolution hasten upon us? Certainly not the laboring men and farmers, but only unprincipled capitalists. It is no fiction, but a notorious fact, the damaging effects of excessive wealth in the hands of private parties and petty corporations upon the country and government. The corporations that plunder the people, openly defy the laws; witness, for instance, the railroad war in Wisconsin.

But one corporation should be allowed to exist, and that the State itself. All corporations are states, and when controlled by a few men are continually making war upon the public welfare. They are only legalized "rings," licensed to defraud and plunder the people. There is not a single corporation in existence except the State, that is not a scourge to the public. Let us look at the objects to be accompolished by a petty corporation, as insurance, for instance. If insurance is a good thing, the lives, and the property of all citizens ought to be insured. Then the State ought to take hold of it. It was so of old, that if the cabin of the back-woodsman was burned, and his rude furniture and household goods destroyed, the neighbors came together and built him a new cabin—a better one, perhaps, than the first, and fitted it up again so that the settler's latter estate was, as a general rule better than his former. Here was practical insurance. So the people as a body should make good the loss of individuals. The State might insure every man's life, and every man's property, and it be little heavier tax upon the public, than the insurance companies levy at present. See the millions (almost) of useless men supported by the public, as insurance agents and officers. The State should see to this magnificent charity, and not leave it to private companies for the "charity" of petty corporations is only to plunder the public, and enrich themselves. Let the office of every corporation (if it be a good office) be assumed by the great corporation—the State—which is responsible directly to the people ; and let no man be permitted to become so rich as to be independent of the people—so rich that he can spend millions to corrupt legislation ; for then he is a petty sovereign, and a practical enemy to American freedom.

These reforms must come, because man is destined to rise to a higher plane of civilization, and with true civilization comes the realization of the highest Christianity. The people are struggling toward emancipation from the thraldom of short-sighted selfishness. We read of attempts at co-operative farming, co-operative factories, etc. This means a willingness that others should be as well off as ourself—a willingness to be equal with our neighbor, and not above him. And then the Trades Unions, and the Grange organizations are educating the people up to a higher and truer love and brotherhood that will become general. Societies and lodges will be merged into the great society—the State—of which all are members, and brethren : a society of mutual helpfulness, of mutual benefits, of mutual love and good will, wherein my neighbor's child will be as dear to me as my own ; and every child will be blessed in my eyes ; and every helpless creature shall have a lodgement in my heart of hearts ; and my love shall be so intense as to shine brightly upon all the little ones of earth and upon all who reach up their hands for help—then will each man be indeed a very Christ of love, radiant with the spirit of the Divine Teacher.

www.ingramcontent.com/pod-product-compliance
Lightning Source LLC
Chambersburg PA
CBHW020241290326
41929CB00045B/1351